LIVING AUTOBIOGRAPHICALLY

LIVING AUTOBIOGRAPHICALLY

How We Create Identity in Narrative

PAUL JOHN EAKIN

CORNELL UNIVERSITY PRESS

ITHACA AND LONDON

Copyright © 2008 by Cornell University

First published 2008 by Cornell University Press
First printing, Cornell Paperbacks, 2008

Printed in the United States of America

Library of Congress Cataloging-in-Publication Data

Eakin, Paul John.
    Living autobiographically : how we create identity in narrative
/ Paul John Eakin.
        p. cm
    Includes bibliographical references and index.
    ISBN 978–0–8014–4724–2 (cloth : alk. paper)–
    ISBN 978–0–8014–7478–1 (pbk. : alk. paper)
    1. Autobiography.   2. Identity (Psychology)   3. Narration
(Rhetoric)   I. Title.

    CT25.E26 2008
    809'.93592—dc22

                                                    2008019570

Cornell University Press strives to use environmentally responsible suppliers and materials to the fullest extent possible in the
publishing of its books. Such materials include vegetable-based,
low-VOC inks and acid-free papers that are recycled, totally
chlorine-free, or partly composed of nonwood fibers. For further
information, visit our website at www.cornellpress.cornell.edu.

Cloth printing   10   9   8   7   6   5   4   3   2   1
Paperback printing   10   9   8   7   6   5   4   3   2   1

In memory of my father
Paul James Eakin
(1904–1980)

CONTENTS

PREFACE

This is a book about narrative and identity, indeed about a connection between them so close that one may speak of narrative identity. The basic proposition here is that narrative is not merely something we tell, listen to, read, or invent; it is an essential part of our sense of who we are.

My thinking about narrative identity, the idea that what we are could be said to be a story of some kind, has developed quite gradually over a long period of time. When I first became interested in autobiographies thirty years ago, I thought of such narratives simply as convenient containers for our life stories. I made a case for the importance of autobiography—then a comparatively neglected kind of literature—by approaching it and the selves that are its primary subject as kinds of fiction. When others took this line much further than I had, treating autobiography as indistinguishable from other kinds of narrative fiction, I found myself dragging my feet. We don't, I feel sure, read autobiographies in the same way that we read novels. Readers take it seriously when autobiographies claim to be based in some sense on biographical and historical fact, so I explored the various registers of fact that come into play in autobiographical texts.

Now, decades later, I see published autobiographies as only the most visible, tangible evidence of the much larger phenomenon that this book seeks to describe, the construction of identity that talking about ourselves and our lives performs in the world. I believe that our life stories are not merely *about* us but in an inescapable and profound way *are* us, at least insofar as we are players in the narrative identity system that structures our current social arrangements—in the United States at any rate.

The first chapter explores the social sources and ethical implications of narrative identity, arguing that when we talk or write about ourselves, we participate in a rule-governed discourse that establishes us as normal individuals in the minds of others. The second chapter presents a neurobiological perspective on self and narrative, proposing that our sense of identity is shaped by our lives in and as bodies. Having laid out these "givens" of narrative identity, I devote the last two chapters to a series of cases that feature individuals (including myself) engaged in fashioning narrative identities. The upshot of my treatment of narrative identity is to suggest that when we say who we are, we draw on—but are not wholly determined by—the physical and social constraints of our lives in human culture. The last chapter proposes that our narrative self-fashioning, oriented as much to the present and future as to the past, may even possess an evolutionary, adaptive value, helping to anchor our shifting identities in time.

The book has, then, a two-part structure: the first part (chapters 1 and 2) identifies the raw materials of the pervasive self-modeling that structures our living, while the second part (chapters 3 and 4) shows this identity work in action. It will be clear in what follows that when I engage what I call the "givens" of narrative identity, I employ two quite distinct perspectives to do so. My approach is social and cultural in chapter 1, whereas my approach in chapter 2 is neurobiological. How and where, one might well ask, do these approaches converge? Insofar as narrative identity is concerned, if the somatic and the cultural come together, I would urge, it is not on the plane of theory but in the lived experience of ordinary individuals telling stories about themselves.[1] Contributing to this claim is my hunch, presented in chapter 2, that there is a link between literary and

---

1. There are critics working today in the emergent field of cognitive literary and cultural studies who do aspire to unite cultural and somatic perspectives in a theoretical synthesis. Ellen Spolsky, e.g., in her preface to *The Work of Fiction: Cognition, Culture, and Complexity,* writes: "It is the deeper understanding of the meaning of context that grounds the possibility of a unified approach to understanding structure and change in both culture and biology, an approach that aims to avoid the reduction to predictability on the one hand, and the chaos of the Borgesian Chinese encyclopedia on the other" (vii). While I remain skeptical about the possibility of the "unified approach" she proposes, I am very much in sympathy with her instinct to explore culture and biology simultaneously. In an earlier book Spolsky comments, "While research in many areas of the humanities and social sciences is concerned ... with understanding the power of culture to structure and

bodily narratives, leading me to argue that self inheres in a narrative of some kind. If this is the case, then the expression of our sense of identity in narrative terms is if anything overdetermined.

Finally, a word about two key terms that appear frequently in the pages that follow: *self* and *identity*. Both words are part of the vocabulary we use to describe key manifestations of our awareness of ourselves as persons, and not surprisingly, given the huge importance of the subject matter at stake, their use and meaning is endlessly discussed and contested, as is the nature of consciousness itself. In *How Our Lives Become Stories* (1999) I approached my concern with the embodied self (about which I will have much more to say in chapter 2) by way of a fivefold model of the nature of selfhood proposed by the psychologist Ulric Neisser in a powerful essay called "Five Kinds of Self-Knowledge." I wrote there that "Neisser's model succeeds, more than any other, in highlighting the primary modes of experience that contribute to the individual's formation of a sense of self" (25). Because Neisser's model provides a useful framework to position my inquiry into narrative identity in this book, I repeat here a brief outline of the five modes of self-experience he distinguishes:

1. The *ecological self:* "The self as perceived with respect to the physical environment; 'I' am the person here in this

---

constrain, it is worthwhile at the same time to investigate the role of biological materialism as co-legislator of human life and understanding" (*Gaps in Nature* 3).

place, engaged in this particular activity" (36). Present in
infancy.

2. The *interpersonal self:* "The self as engaged in immediate
   unreflective social interaction with another person" (41);
   "'I' am the person who is engaged, here, in this particular
   human interchange" (36). Present in infancy.

3. The *extended self:* the self of memory and anticipation, the
   self existing outside the present moment; "I am the person who had certain specific experiences, who regularly
   engages in certain specific and familiar routines" (36).
   By the age of three, children are aware of themselves "as
   existing outside the present moment, and hence of the
   extended self" (47).

4. The *private self:* the self of "conscious experiences that
   are not available to anyone else" (50); "I am, in principle,
   the only person who can feel this unique and particular
   pain" (36). Although experts differ as to the emergence of
   this sense of privacy in developmental chronology, many
   studies show children as "aware of the privacy of mental
   life before the age of 5" (50).

5. The *conceptual self:* the extremely diverse forms of self-
   information—social roles, personal traits, theories of
   body and mind, of subject and person—that posit the
   self as a category, either explicitly or implicitly. (Neisser's
   discrimination of five primary kinds of self-information,
   of course, is one such conceptual model.) (Eakin, *How
   Our Lives Become Stories* 22–23; page references are to
   Neisser's article).[2]

---

2. See Eakin, *How Our Lives Become Stories* 22–25 for a more detailed discussion of Neisser's model.

Clearly, for Neisser, and for me as well, when it comes to subjectivity, *self* is the umbrella term, and I shall argue in chapter 2, drawing on recent work in neurobiology, that the self-experience Neisser theorizes is deeply implicated in some form at every level of consciousness. *Identity,* by contrast, is one manifestation of Neisser's fifth mode, the "conceptual self." It refers to the version of ourselves that we display not only to others but also to ourselves whenever we have occasion to reflect on or otherwise engage in self-characterization. Whenever I variously think of myself, for example, as a literary critic, a father, a midwesterner, a bourgeois suburbanite, and so forth, I am thinking of myself in terms of identity. *Self,* then, is the larger, more comprehensive term for the totality of our subjective experience. As I shall suggest in chapter 1, our identities may erode, but we remain selves of some kind as long as consciousness continues.

ACKNOWLEDGMENTS

Portions of this book were published elsewhere in somewhat different versions, and this material is used with permission here. These publications include: "Autobiography and the Value Structures of Ordinary Experience: Marianne Gullestad's *Everyday Life Philosophers*," *Making Meaning of Narratives*, ed. Ruthellen Josselson and Amia Lieblich, *The Narrative Study of Lives* 6 (Thousand Oaks, CA: Sage, 1999), 25–43; "Breaking Rules: The Consequences of Self-Narration," *Biography: An Interdisciplinary Quarterly* 24 (2001): 113–27; "Living Autobiographically," *Biography: An Interdisciplinary Quarterly* 28 (2005): 1–14; "What Are We Reading When We Read Autobiography?" *Narrative* 12 (2004): 121–32; "Selfhood, Autobiography, and Interdisciplinary Inquiry: A Reply to George Butte," *Narrative* 13 (2005): 310–14; "Narrative Identity and Narrative

Imperialism: A Response to Galen Strawson and James Phelan," *Narrative* 14 (2006): 180–87; and "The Economy of Narrative Identity," Supplement to *History of Political Economy* 39 (2007): 117–33.

I record here my thanks to many people—inviters, listeners, readers, editors—who helped me sharpen my thinking about narrative identity: William L. Andrews, Oya Berk, Rudolf Dekker, Paul Dudenhefer, Isabel Duran, Susanna Egan, Janet Ellerby, Victoria Elmwood, Evelyn Forget, Sherrill Grace, Marianne Gullestad, Norman Holland, Alfred Hornung, Craig Howes, Jessica Luck, David Parker, James P. Phelan, Roger Porter, Angelo Righetti, the late Eric Schocket, Norma Thompson, Barbara Waxman, and Roy Weintraub. A timely nudge from Jeffrey Wallen helped me out of a stall in writing this book. G. Thomas Couser, John Schilb, and Eugene L. Stelzig gave me expert advice about my manuscript. J. D. Scrimgeour coached me on writing personal narrative, as did supportive colleagues at a symposium in Honolulu organized by John Barbour, Richard Freadman, and Eugene L. Stelzig. Thanks, too, to members of the faculty Life Writing Seminar at the Indiana University Institute for Advanced Study, with whom I discussed my work along the way. Naming these names reminds me how much I have profited from my friends and colleagues in bringing this project to conclusion.

I owe special thanks to Peter J. Potter, Editor-in-Chief at Cornell University Press, for his support of this project.

Thanks, too, to my copyeditor Emily Votruba and to Ange Romeo-Hall, who guided the book through production.

As always, Sybil S. Eakin remains my best critic.

PAUL JOHN EAKIN

Bloomington, Indiana

LIVING AUTOBIOGRAPHICALLY

CHAPTER 1

TALKING ABOUT OURSELVES

The Rules of the Game

We tell stories about ourselves every day. Sometimes we can get other people to listen to them, but even when we can't, at any given moment this process of self-narration is constantly unfolding in our heads, in however loose and disorderly a fashion. In a certain sense we are always talking about ourselves to ourselves if to no one else, making plans about what we're going to do, reviewing what we have done and thought and felt. This talking in our heads is the primary content of what the psychologist William James taught us more than a hundred years ago to call the stream of consciousness. More recently, the neurologist Oliver Sacks has made as bold a claim for the function of this self-narration in our lives as any I have ever encountered: "It might be said that each of us constructs and lives a 'narrative,' and that this narrative *is* us, our identities" (*The Man Who Mistook* 110, emphasis in original).

Sacks's observation was prompted by the plight of a brain-damaged individual suffering from severe memory loss. Because the patient, "Mr. Thompson," could not remember who he was for more than a minute or two at most, he spent his waking hours in frenetic self-invention, seeking to construct new identities to take the place of old ones that he forgot as soon as he created them. For Sacks, Mr. Thompson's condition exposes identity's twin supporting structures, memory and narrative: What is this man without his story? I keep returning to the nagging puzzle raised by this disturbing case, the radical equivalence Sacks proposes between narrative and identity, between the stories we tell about ourselves and who we really are.

If Sacks is right, and I am convinced that he is, then talking about ourselves involves a lot more than self-indulgence; when we do it, we perform a work of self-construction. The very phrase "talking about/ourselves" tends to separate selfhood from the act of expressing it, to attribute an independent existence to the "ourselves" we would be "talking about," whereas the "talking," I argue, actually calls our narrative identities into being; there is a mutually enhancing interplay between what we are and what we say we are. In speaking of *narrative identity* in the pages that follow, I propose, as Sacks does, an extremely close and dynamic relation between narrative and identity, for narrative is not only a literary form but part of the fabric of our lived experience. When it comes to our identities, narrative is not merely *about* self, but is rather in some profound way a constituent part *of* self. In this chapter I explore the social sources and ethical implications of this notion of narrative identity.

Jolting Events

"This narrative *is* us, our identities"—surely the idea that what we are is a story of some kind is counterintuitive and even extravagant. Don't we know that we are more than that, that Sacks can't be right? And our instinctive recoil points to an important truth: there are many modes of self and self-experience, more than could possibly be represented in the kind of self-narration Sacks refers to, more than any autobiography could relate. Developmental psychologists convince me, though, that we are trained as children to attach special importance to one kind of selfhood, that of the extended self, so much so that we do in fact regard it as identity's signature. The term *extended self* comes from the psychologist Ulric Neisser, who has identified at least five kinds of selfhood, involving physical, social, and mental contexts.[1] It is Neisser's extended self, the self of memory and anticipation, the self existing continuously across time, that is the primary subject of autobiographical discourse. According to Neisser, by the age of three, children are aware of themselves "as existing outside the present moment, and hence of the extended self" (47). It is this temporal dimension of extended selfhood that lends itself to expression in narrative form of the kind Sacks posits as identity's core, for narrative is especially suited to registering the effects of time and change that are central to this mode of self-experience. As a result, the extended self takes the form of a narrative identity, and identity narratives serve as the medium

---

1. See the preface where I present Neisser's five kinds of selfhood.

for displaying that self in interpersonal encounters.[2] For others, we are indeed versions of the extended self and its identity story; when we perform these stories, we establish ourselves for others as normal individuals—something that Mr. Thompson tried to do, and failed.

If this picture of narrative identity I have sketched is correct, autobiography is not merely something we read in a book; rather, as a discourse of identity, delivered bit by bit in the stories we tell about ourselves day in and day out, autobiography structures our living. We don't, though, tend to give much thought to this process of self-narration precisely because, after years of practice, we do it so well. When this identity story practice is disrupted, however, we can be jolted into awareness of the central role it plays in organizing our social world. I want to consider two events that had this jolting power for me.

First, September 11. The erection of a viewing platform at Ground Zero in lower Manhattan in the months following the disaster testified to the desire of ordinary people to see for themselves what happened on that day. But how to see it? We are by now all too familiar with the devastating images of the towers' collapse, but in addition to this cataclysmic material event, in the days that followed we had to reckon with the grievous rent in the social fabric produced by the sudden death of nearly three thousand people. This social dimension of the catastrophe is harder to see, but

2. See Ricoeur, *Time and Narrative,* for an elaborate account of narrative as a temporal form.

I think that when the *New York Times* created "A Nation Challenged," a special daily section that chronicled the aftermath of September 11, the paper helped us to envision what cannot be seen from the viewing platform: the network of selves and lives that supported the world of the towers every bit as much as the columns of steel that buckled in the conflagration's immense heat.

Anchoring each edition of "A Nation Challenged" on its final page were the "Portraits of Grief," brief evocations of the lives of those killed at the World Trade Center. Why did so many people tell me they had read these portraits with intense fascination? I know I did. Yet for most readers, the victims were neither friends nor relations, nor were they public figures. When the faceless statistics of the missing are given a face, a name, a story, we respond, I think, not only to the individualism that is so strong a feature in American culture, but also, I would urge, to an instinctive reflex to heal the rupture in these lives that we accept as somehow representative of our own.[3] As Howell Raines, then editor in chief of the *Times,* observed in an interview on National Public Radio, the portraits are "snapshots" of lives "interrupted": "They give you a sense of the living person," he said. With a huge investment of money and labor involving more than eighty reporters, the paper attempted to recover something of those lives, performing symbolically a work of repair that paralleled the clearing of the rubble at Ground Zero. The

3. On September 11, 2006 the *Times* published a follow-up to the "Portraits of Grief" project to record how some of the bereaved were dealing with "the healing process." See "Revisiting the Families."

magnitude of the project is arresting: more than eighteen hundred portraits had been published by the end of 2001.[4]

What do these "snapshots" of "interrupted" lives look like? There were usually a dozen or more of them on the page, with a banner headline across the top announcing some of the headings of the individual profiles, as, for example, this one from November 17, 2001: "A Taste for Fine Wine, a Seeker of Good Deals, and Fun on Halloween." The single large photograph that invariably headed the page—usually a picture of some makeshift urban shrine to the missing or else a burial scene—captured the commemorative intention behind the portraits arranged in columns below. Yet the portraits, striking in their informality, were clearly not obituaries in any usual sense, nor were they eulogies. The header for each piece featured some leading characteristic, a kind of capsule identity or microstory: "The Gadget Guru," "A Motorcycle for a Ring," "Always Time for Golf." The short paragraphs that followed, touching on personal qualities, habits, favorite activities, and plans, highlighted life plots now left incomplete. Ironies and fateful choices abounded. The loose narrative fragments were exactly like the ephemeral bits and pieces of the stories we tell about ourselves every day, and this is not surprising, for the portraits were generated in conversations between reporters and those close to the deceased. They displayed

4. In fact, on December 31, 2001, the *Times* published in a composite double-page spread a list of all the names of the victims whose sketches had appeared in the "Portraits" project up to that date, a wall of names on the order of Maya Lin's Vietnam memorial on the Mall in Washington, D.C. See "A Nation Challenged."

with striking immediacy the scraps of identity narrative that make up all forms of self-narration and life writing. In characterizing these "portraits" as "loose," "informal," and "fragmentary," I mean to suggest just how close they are to the *spoken* exchanges in which we transact our narrative identities. The novelty of the "portraits" is precisely a consequence of the ordinariness of the identity material they present, an ordinariness that accounts for the fact that there was no preexisting written genre to capture it—why, indeed, should this material be preserved? "Small talk," we call it. What we say about ourselves in passing is usually swept away, the detritus of discourse, and it takes a rupture in the normal unfolding of everyday life to bring it into view and remind us of its value as identity's bedrock. The "Portraits of Grief" pages offer a viewing platform, as it were, from which we can glimpse in a freeze-frame what our narratively constructed identities might look like in the aggregate. We see, cumulatively, a veritable anthology of the models of identity and life story current in our culture; the homeliness, the familiarity, of this identity narrative material is deeply moving precisely because we use it to talk about ourselves every day. If the "Portraits of Grief" suggest what the narrative identity system, rendered in memorable shorthand, looks like when it is functioning normally, what does it look like when it breaks down altogether?

Picture an old man in a wheelchair clutching a teddy bear, an old man who has forgotten who he is, an old man no one else seems to know. This was John Kingery's plight, and I remember that when I read his disturbing story in the

Times some years ago, it conjured up the fate that might await us all if our social identities should become unmoored from their narrative anchor in autobiographical memory. The front-page article reported that this eighty-two-year-old man had been abandoned at a dog-racing track in Idaho: "A typewritten note pinned to his chest identified him as 'John King,' an Alzheimer's patient in need of care. He was wearing bedroom slippers and a sweatshirt that said 'Proud to be an American.' The labels on his new clothing had been cut away, and all identifying markers on his wheelchair were removed" (Egan). Identity theft squared, I thought. As it turned out, one of Kingery's daughters, who had been appropriating his pension and Social Security checks, had dumped him at the track; then a second daughter from an earlier marriage, reading her father's story in the paper, flew to his rescue. While the *Times* reporter's angle on the Kingery case was "parent-dumping," for me this man's story was his lack of story—for a time, no one knew who he was. Are we diminished as persons, I wondered, when we can no longer say who we are? And while we can, what are our ethical responsibilities toward those who can't? The hard lesson of our population's increasing longevity is that more and more of us will live to witness if not to experience for ourselves what it is like to become de-storied individuals.

The Case against Narrative Identity

Thinking about the "Portraits of Grief" and John Kingery's story, I see many reasons to believe that what we are could be said to be a narrative of some kind. In an essay titled "Against Narrativity," however, the philosopher Galen Strawson has dismissed the idea of narrative identity as merely an "intellectual fashion" (439) currently in vogue among academics. He, for one, reports that he has "absolutely no sense of [his] life as a narrative with form, or indeed as a narrative without form" and no "great or special interest in [his] past." Why indeed would he be interested in his past, he goes on to say, when he can say of his sense of "self," "I have no significant sense that *I*—the I now considering this question—was there in the further past" (433). Strawson consistently—and mistakenly—assumes as he does here that a sense of one's life as a narrative of some kind is exclusively the consequence of one's having a sense of continuous identity, a sense that the person one is now is in some way the same as the person one has been at earlier stages of one's life. For Strawson it seems to follow, then, that if your sense of identity is discontinuous, you will be indifferent to narrative formulations of your identity's story. Is this in fact the case? I think not, but let's consider discontinuous identity as Strawson models it, for this is the basis for his resistance to the idea that narrative can provide a primary structure for our experience of selfhood.

Although Strawson does not disavow his possession of autobiographical memories nor their "from-the-inside character" (434) (that sense of immediacy and particularity that are the hallmarks of firsthand eyewitness experience), he insists that he cannot access previous identity states; he cannot reexperience or reinhabit them. Distinguishing with an asterisk the "I" and "me" of his present self from those of his past, he concludes: "So: it's clear to me that events in my remoter past didn't happen to me*" (433). Strawson's statement here may be arresting, as I suspect he intends, but in fact it merely echoes a commonplace sentiment in the literature of autobiography. Henry James (whom he cites by way of illustration), Malcolm X, Christa Wolf—these are only a few of the many autobiographers who insist on their experience of discontinuous identity, the sense that they are not now who they were. There is both psychological and neurological support for this view. The novelist and auto-biographer David Malouf makes this penetrating observation about the impossibility of recapturing earlier, *embodied* selves:

> That body is out of reach. And it isn't simply a matter of its being forgotten in us—of a failure of memory or imagination to summon it up, but of a change in perceiving itself. What moving back into it would demand is an act of *un*-remembering, a dismantling of the body's experience that would be a kind of dying, a casting off, one by one, of all the tissues of perception, conscious and not, through which our very notion of body has been remade. (64, emphasis in original)

As Malouf suggests, consciousness is not a neutral medium in which memories can be replayed and the past repeated intact. While we may have the sensation that we are capable of reliving the past—Vladimir Nabokov, Marcel Proust, Nathalie Sarraute, and many other autobiographers have claimed they could—research in brain studies offers no support for belief in invariant memory or belief in the possibility of re-experiencing earlier states of selfhood. Nearly twenty years ago the neurologist Israel Rosenfield argued that memories share the constructed nature of all brain events: "Recollection is a kind of perception,...*and every context will alter the nature of what is recalled*" (89, emphasis added).[5] So if it is true, strictly speaking, that we are not now who we were and that we can never hope to repeat the past in any absolute sense, does it then follow that the idea of narrative identity and the life story that would feature it become irrelevant to our lived experience of selfhood? Why does Strawson think so?

Generalizing from his own experience of discontinuous identity, Strawson posits that all human beings belong to one of two distinct "styles of temporal being" (430), which he terms the Episodic and the Diachronic. Episodics, such as himself, believe that their identity states are discontinuous: Because their sense of self in any present bears no obvious

---

5. Yet consider the testimony of persons who have experienced a deep trauma of some kind and who report the sensation of literally repeating past consciousness. Describing his research in the Fortunoff Archive for Holocaust Testimonies at Yale, Geoffrey Hartman cites the case of Jolly Z., who was asked what she sees when she is "back there." "Struggling for words, and still not entirely present," Hartman writes, "she answers: 'I'm not here....I don't even know about myself now. I'm there...somebody else talks out of me....You see it's not me. It's that person who experienced it who is talking about those experiences'" (ellipses in original). Hartman comments: "An entire phenomenology of traumatic memory is encapsulated in statements like these." Unlike the more usual stance of the individual engaged in recollection who, as Malouf suggests, needs somehow to traverse the gulf that separates the past from the present, Hartman's victim of trauma is already "back there"; so completely is she inhabited by that earlier identity state that she can say, "I'm not here." (The testimony of Jolly Z. quoted by Hartman appears in Kraft 22.)

connection to their sense of self at any previous point in their history (they are not now who they were), their selves and lives are never organized in narrative form. In sharp contrast, Strawson's Diachronics believe that their identity states are continuous (they *are* in some sense who they were), and they can see their selves and lives accordingly in consecutive narrative terms. I say "believe" advisedly, because Strawson never makes clear whether he is describing a given of felt experience or an attitude toward it. He asserts that "the fundamentals of temporal temperament are genetically determined" (431); however, although he states that his Episodic and Diachronic categories are "radically opposed" (430), he describes himself as only "relatively Episodic" (433). It is hard to know, then, given this wobble in Strawson's thinking, just how seriously one should take his identity categories; but the case he makes against narrative identity is instructive and worth a further hearing.

So how *do* individuals sort out into Strawson's Diachronic and Episodic categories? I think that Strawson is correct in his belief that most people would identify themselves as Diachronics—that is, if they ever gave much thought to such identity questions, and they probably don't. I think most people probably believe in continuous identity at some level, and they probably think of their lives in developmental terms. Do they believe, with Wordsworth, that "the Child is Father of the Man"? Well, sure. But, as with opinion polls, the answers you get to a question depend on how it is asked. If you ask people whether they believe in continuous identity, most, as Strawson reports, will say they do. If you ask them, though, about the extent to which they can call up the past, about whether they can actually reinhabit earlier periods of their lives, pressing them as to whether they can in the present reexperience earlier states of consciousness, I suspect that many of these previously unreflecting Diachronics would admit to being Episodics too. My hunch is that most of us probably belong in part to both camps.

The primary weakness of Strawson's case against narrative identity is that his Episodic and Diachronic categories, in addition to their intrinsic instability, simply do not connect coherently and predictably with a narrative outlook on experience. Strawson himself seems to admit as much when he comments, "I've made some distinctions, but none of them cut very sharply" (446).[6] Many an Episodic turned autobiographer, for example, including writers such as Henry James, Virginia Woolf, and Stendhal (all of whom Strawson cites as models of the Episodic type), *do* take a narrative interest in their experience. For a characteristic instance, take John Updike. He definitely fits the Episodic profile: "Each day, we wake slightly altered, and the person we were yesterday is dead" (221). Yet he proceeds in *Self-Consciousness: Memoirs* to reconstruct his past in narrative to recover something of those earlier selves. That is to say that Episodics may have a special motive for an interest in narrative precisely *because* they are Episodics.

6. See James Battersby, who systematically dismantles Strawson's binary thinking and concludes that "we should then reject his whole scheme, eliminating in the process any concern about aligning ourselves on one side or the other of the Diachronic/Episodic divide" (42).

It is time for full disclosure: Strawson, I infer, is radically different from me when it comes to the rhythms of consciousness, which in my case, sleeping and waking, are invariably narrative in cast. Most mornings I wake with relief from agitated dreams and their puzzling plots, only to resume, as William James suggests we do, the unfolding of my own stream of consciousness, which, despite astonishing jolts and cuts as memory jumps from one time frame to another, pulls to a steadily invented story line of present and future plans. In sharp contrast, Strawson celebrates a fleeting and absolute present—"what I care about . . . is how I am now" (438)—and he invokes an eighteenth-century English philosopher, the Earl of Shaftesbury, as the patron saint of this Episodic mode:

> [But] what matter for memory? . . . If, *whilst I am,* I am as I should be, what do I care more? And thus let me lose *self* every hour, and be twenty successive selfs, or new selfs, 'tis all one to me: so [long as] I lose not my opinion [i.e., my overall outlook, my character, my moral identity]. (quoted in Strawson 438, emphasis in original)

What would it be like to live without memory? What would it be like to lose one's "self" every hour, indeed every few seconds? Think back to Oliver Sacks's Mr. Thompson, the man whose memory had been gravely damaged by Korsakoff's syndrome. In Mr. Thompson Sacks portrays an Episodic in extremis, an individual who *"must literally make himself (and his world) up every moment."* As we have seen, it is this man's desperate condition that prompts Sacks to reflect on the narrative anchor of human identity, observing that "each of us constructs and lives a 'narrative,' and that this narrative *is* us, our identities" (*The Man Who Mistook* 110, emphasis in original). (This is the same formulation of narrative identity, by the way, that Strawson quotes and attacks in "Against Narrativity.") The clinical context of Sacks's observation is instructive and sobering. Note that Mr. Thompson, unlike Strawson, doesn't enjoy the safety net of a sense of himself as a "human being taken as a whole," that sense of continuous identity that underwrites Strawson's comfortable claim of discontinuous identity. Strawson's brief for the Episodic life, which he characterizes as "truly happy-go-lucky, see-what-comes-along" (449), strikes me as breezy and untested. To be sure, who is to say that Mr. Thompson is not a happy man? Who would judge him to be diminished as a person? Strawson, I take it, would not, for he rightly opposes an ethics that would link narrative capacity and personhood. But would he—or the Earl of Shaftesbury—really want to *be* Mr. Thompson? Perhaps, but I have never encountered anyone who did not hope that memory and the sense of life story it supports would survive intact to the end. In my experience, most people fear memory loss and the death of the extended self that follows from it—witness the widespread anxiety about Alzheimer's disease and aging in the United States today. It is this fear that Sacks captures when he wonders whether loss of memory entails loss of identity: "Has [Mr. Thompson] been pithed, scooped-out, de-souled, by disease?" (*Man* 113).

I think that Strawson is mistaken when he attributes the dominance of the idea of narrative identity to "intellectual fashion." What he fails to reckon with is that we are embedded in a narrative identity system whether we like it or not. Our social arrangements—in the United States, at least—assume that we all have narrative identities and that we can display them on demand. I should emphasize that I regard this narrative identity situation as both culture specific and period specific, although I suspect that something like it obtains and has obtained in many times and places. Two clarifications are in order here. First, with respect to *culture,* a counter that one needs to use with care when speaking of particular cases: the anthropologist Marianne Gullestad, whose work I will present in some detail in chapter 3, cautions that individuals today may belong to several "partcultures" simultaneously ("Reflections" 18–20). She advocates accordingly a concept of culture that is sufficiently supple to address the complexities of contemporary life, "reconfigur[ing] it as a set of permeable, less bounded, and less tightly integrated structures and practices" (14). I think her notion of partcultures is very useful: the divide between the world of work and the world of home would be only the most obvious illustration of our daily encounters with partcultures and their requirements. My second clarification, about which I'll have more to say later on in this chapter, is that various factors—of gender, of class, of race and ethnicity—inflect our socialization into the narrative practices of our settings.

My claim that we are players willy-nilly in a narrative identity system may seem surprising and counterintuitive, given that we doubtless believe that we talk about ourselves both freely and spontaneously. Don't we conduct our lives, after all, in a culture of democratic individualism? In fact, the language we use when we present ourselves and our stories to others is a rule-governed discourse, both when we talk and when we write. Because the rules that govern our self-reporting are more obviously visible in the case of written narratives, I will look first at a conveniently prominent example from the world of mass media and public life. Then I will show that when we talk about ourselves, in however fragmentary, spontaneous, and casual a fashion, we are also operating under the discipline of a rule-grounded identity regime. In both writing and speaking we can get into trouble for breaking the rules.

Truth or Consequences on *Oprah*

It is hard to imagine how autobiography's usually tacit conventions could have been given greater exposure than they were in the case of James Frey's memoir, *A Million Little Pieces,* which was adopted by Oprah Winfrey's Book Club in the fall of 2005. The controversy over this book, which erupted a few months later, caught my attention on Tuesday, January 10, 2006. In an article in the *New York Times* titled "Best-Selling Memoir Draws Scrutiny" (Wyatt), I learned that a website suitably named The Smoking Gun had posted a critique of Frey's story on January 8, charging that he had "wholly fabricated or wildly embellished details of his purported criminal career." The initial response from Doubleday, Frey's publisher, reported on January 11 in the

Times under the heading "When A Memoir And Facts Collide" (Wyatt), was dismissive: by Doubleday's permissive definition, in a memoir, anything goes—it is the author's call. But that same night, the author was called to account on CNN's *Larry King Live*. Quizzed by King, Frey conceded that he had made up some details, but he stood by the basic truth of his story, namely, "that he was an alcoholic and drug addict who overcame his addiction" (Wyatt, "Writer"). Moreover, Oprah Winfrey called in to Larry King during the show to express her continuing faith in Frey and his "underlying message of redemption" (quoted in Dowd). As Maureen Dowd's column put it a couple of days later: "Oprah! How Could Ya?" And on the 13th, the *Times* ran an editorial on Frey titled simply "Call It Fiction."

Just when I thought that the Frey flap was running out of gas, if anything, it picked up speed in the following days. By this point, the story was popping up everywhere in columns, letters, and cartoons. On Sunday, January 15, one week after the Smoking Gun posting, the *Times*'s lead story in the Week in Review section featured a wide-ranging discussion of autobiographical truth under the title "My True Story, More or Less, And Maybe Not at All" (Kennedy). That same Sunday, on the op-ed pages, Mary Karr, author herself of two outstanding memoirs, wrote a scathing attack on Frey titled "His So-Called Life." "Call me outdated," she announced, "but I want to stay hamstrung by objective truth." "Distinguishing between fiction and non- isn't nearly the taxing endeavor some would have us believe," Karr commented scornfully, "sexing a chicken is way harder."

Frey's story took a darker turn in its second week of intense media scrutiny. Recovering addicts weighed in on the inaccuracies of his account of life in a treatment center, although Doubleday found a couple of the recovered to stand up for its battered author. More damaging were the columns about the Frey affair by Michiko Kakutani (on the 17th) and by Frank Rich (on the 22nd). They saw something more disturbing in the Frey case than the unmasking of a mediocre talent who had aspired to be in the same league as Hemingway, Kerouac, and Mailer. Interpreting Frey's success as the culmination of what she called "the memoir craze" and the popularity of "recovery-movement reminiscences," Michiko Kakutani argued that it illustrates the culture's pernicious drift toward relativism, a bending of the truth that creates a climate in which the existence of the Holocaust can be questioned. In "Truthiness 101: From Frey to Alito," Frank Rich castigated Frey and his book as exemplars of what the Comedy Central star Stephen Colbert had called "truthiness." In an age of spinning, the winners are those with the slickest stories: "It's the truthiness of all those imminent mushroom clouds that sold the invasion of Iraq," Rich observed.

The climax of the Frey story came, fittingly, on *The Oprah Winfrey Show* on January 26, and it made the front page of the *Times* the following day: "Live on 'Oprah,' a Memoirist Is Kicked Out of the Book Club" (Wyatt). In addition to Frey and herself, Winfrey had assembled a large supporting cast that included Nan Talese (Frey's publisher at Doubleday) and columnists Dowd and Rich. Winfrey expressed her contrition for the mistake she said she had made when she called in to Larry King to support Frey, which she feared had left the impression that she was indifferent to the truth. Winfrey then rebuked Frey for deceiving her and her book club's readers; she rebuked his publisher as well for not properly vetting the book. "You lied," she told Frey bluntly. Truth or consequences, as they say: on January 30, Frey's film deal was in trouble ("Studio Has Second Thoughts"), and by the end of February I read that his book deals were also falling through ("Riverhead Books Pulls Out of James Frey Deal").

Text, person, culture—the Frey case put three questions into play: What kind of book is *A Million Little Pieces*? Who is James Frey, really? And what kind of culture promotes a man like this and such a book? What the Frey episode confirms is that the reception of memoir is contractual: readers expect autobiographers to exhibit some basic respect for the truth of their lives—break that trust and suffer the consequences. And who, then, is the arbiter of autobiographical truth? Clearly not the author in this case—Frey was totally unreliable. And clearly not the editor and publisher—Nan Talese's notion of memoir was self-serving, a lame attempt at damage control. Oprah Winfrey, then, or The Smoking Gun? In the last analysis, readers, individually and collectively, monitored the memoir's claims to truth. In this instance, to be sure, the author and his publishers gamed the generic system and made a temporary killing. The Frey controversy did turn out to be about packaging:

○ about the definition of a literary genre (the author eventually confided that he had discussed with his agent and

publishers whether to market his book as a novel or a memoir);
- ○ about the author's identity (had he really led the criminal life he said he had? etc.);
- ○ about the values of the culture at large (truth or "truth-iness").

Whereas we probably don't learn much about the novel as a kind of writing from reading the newspaper, in the case of autobiography, we do. Why is that? Because autobiography is a referential art: it self-consciously, usually explicitly, positions itself with reference to the world, and when it does so, it invites—at least potentially—the kind of scrutiny that Frey's book in fact received. We can write about our lives in a memoir as we like, but we can't expect to be read as we like—not, at any rate, if we flout the conventions, and in the case of autobiography, telling the truth is the cardinal rule. Readers cut memoirists plenty of slack when they are having fun, and that includes readers of Mary Karr and Frank McCourt. *The Liars' Club* and *Angela's Ashes* feature unusually vivid and hugely extended accounts of the authors' lives as quite young children—pages and pages reporting verbatim dialogue that young Frank would have overheard at ages three, four, and five; 170 pages describing Mary Karr's life at age seven. Call this fiction, call it imaginative reconstruction; these writers impress us as trying to tell the fundamental biographical truth of their lives. As Karr puts it memorably, "I want to stay hamstrung by objective truth." But cross the line, as James Frey confesses he did, and the memoirist gets kicked out of the book club. Breaking trust with the readers

of your memoir, moreover, proves to be a potentially action-
able offense: in September of 2006, Frey and his publisher
apparently agreed to recompense readers who filed lawsuits
claiming they had been defrauded when they bought *A Million Little Pieces.*[7]

The Narrative Identity System

Talking about ourselves is also a kind of genre, as it turns
out, with rules and penalties that bear on our recognition
by others as persons; as with memoir, so in self-narration,
the culture's fundamental values are at stake. Despite our
illusions of autonomy and self-determination—"*I* write my
story, *I* say who I am"—we do not invent our identities out
of whole cloth. Instead, we draw on the resources of the cultures we inhabit to shape them, resources that specify what
it means to be a man, a woman, a worker, a person in the settings where we live our lives. It is easy enough to posit that
we draw on models of identity as we go about the business of
making our selves, whether in our lives or in writing about
them; it is much more challenging, however, to specify how
this process works, especially because I think our practice of
self-construction is largely unconscious.

7. See Motoko Rich. As of November 2007, 1,729 people have asked Frey's
publisher to reimburse them for buying the memoir. Although the claims for re-
imbursement so far have cost only $27,348, Random House has paid $783,000 in
legal fees and another $432,000 in costs related to the settlement. See "A Few Little
Pieces."

If even our casual conversation about ourselves is regulated by conventions, why aren't we more consciously and explicitly aware of them? To begin with, the habitual, daily performance of self-narration tends to mask the fact that we participate in a rule-governed system; after years of practice, we operate on automatic pilot; we know the identity protocols by heart. The working of the system becomes visible, however, when memory fails and narrative competence collapses, or when self-narration is deliberately refused. Then the link between identity narrative and normality becomes manifest. As Kay Young and Jeffrey Saver put it bluntly in their study "The Neurology of Narrative": "Individuals who have lost the ability to construct narrative...have lost their selves." We can test their view against our own experience, for most of us have encountered individuals whose memories and narrative competence have been impaired by injury, disease, or failing powers—it is an increasingly common occurrence in an aging population such as our own.

The refusal of self-narration offers an equally revealing if rarer insight into the operation and social significance of narrative identity. William Chaloupka uses the case of the Hood River "John Doe" to illustrate Michel Foucault's understanding of the link between the individual and the apparatuses of state power. Here was a man, arrested for stealing a car, who refused to tell police in Hood River, Oregon, anything about himself, even his name. Training a Foucauldian lens on this otherwise minor episode, Chaloupka concludes that "the act of autobiographical telling has roots and functions crucial to the operations of contemporary power" (378).

John Doe's refusal to identify himself disrupted customary grids of identity processing, making them instructively visible as a result. The bafflement of the police in dealing with this anomalous situation points up how the judicial system normally functions. According to a local paper, John Doe "would probably have been out of jail already had he cooperated with authorities." "Without a past," the paper comments, "no one could determine if Doe was a risk to flee the area" (cited in Chaloupka 373). John Doe was eventually identified by his father, who had seen a picture of his son circulated by the police. "Soon after his name was discovered," Chaloupka reports, "[he] was sentenced to ninety days in jail and was promptly released on probation, as he had already served far more than ninety days" (388).

Whether we are considering a contrarian John Doe or our forgetful elders, lapses in identity narration generate consequences, including possible confinement in prisons or long-term care facilities. These consequences confirm that the interpersonal exchange of self-narrations is a rule-governed regime and that the rules are enforced. Others police our performance, and it is also true that we do this policing ourselves. We monitor and judge what others tell us (we exchange glances, we may even roll our eyes); we determine that our interlocutor is "not tracking," has "lost it," and so forth. The psychologist John Shotter claims that our participation in what I am calling a narrative identity system is governed by "social accountability": "What we talk of *as* our experience of our reality is constituted for us very largely by the *already established* ways in which we *must* talk in our attempts to *account* for ourselves—and for it—to the others around us.... And only certain ways of talking are deemed legitimate" (141, emphasis in original). The analyses of Chaloupka, Foucault, and Shotter sensitize us to the presence of social constraint in the exercise of self-narration; our sense of autonomy, of total control, is something of an illusion when it comes to talking about ourselves. The source of our narrative identities, they propose, is not some mysterious interiority, but other people.

How do we know how to play this narrative identity game? Training in self-narration begins early, and the fact that it does testifies to our tacit complicity in the working of the system. We introduce our children to the practice of making identity narrative during an unusually rich phase of early childhood development in which the child's newly acquired language and narrative skills combine with temporal awareness and a nascent sense of social accountability to lay the foundations of autobiographical memory. This training takes the form of what psychologists call the child's "memory talk," homely little stories that parents and caregivers coach us to tell about ourselves. The early materials of these collaborative efforts in making a life story are slight, to be sure—a walk around the block, activities at nursery school, a trip to the zoo—but they provide practice nonetheless for longer, solo flights of self-narration in the time to come. In these parent-child conversations "children learn the conventionalized narrative forms that eventually provide a structure for internally represented memories" (Fivush and Reese 115). Describing this process of socialization,

Robyn Fivush offers this memorable formulation of the give-and-take between awareness of self and autobiographical memory: "The self-concept and memories of past experiences develop dialectically and begin to form a life history. The life history, in turn, helps organize both memories of past experiences and the self-concept" (Fivush 280–81). Children learn not only that they are expected to be able to display to others autobiographical memories arranged in narrative form; they learn what is tellable as well.[8]

Lest my account of the child's initiation into what I am calling a narrative identity system seem to predicate a one-size-fits-all model of narrative practices, I should point out that research into "memory talk" offers a quite nuanced picture of this phase of a child's socialization. With regard to gender, for example, Robyn Fivush and Elaine Reese identify two "distinct parental styles for talking about the past," an "elaborative," discursive style, and a "repetitive," utilitarian style. "Elaborative" parents "tend to have long conversations in which they embellish aspects of the story and generally provide a richly detailed and progressive account of events" (Fivush and Reese 119), whereas "repetitive" parents "tend to have short conversations with their children about the past," repeating "the same questions over and over in an attempt to prompt the child into giving the 'correct' answer" (121). Fivush and Reese are intrigued to note that "parents tend to be more elaborative with daughters than

8. For a more extended treatment of narrative identity and the emergence of the extended self in early childhood, see Eakin, *How Our Lives Become Stories* 102–23.

with sons" (125), and they conclude that "males and females have different preferred modes of thinking about and talking about the past, but can switch styles depending on the context" (127).

It is also true that class is equally a player when it comes to training the young child how to talk about the past. Assuming that "selves vary substantially within and across cultures," Angela Wiley and her colleagues investigate personal storytelling "as a medium through which European American youngsters begin to construct selves that bear the imprint of an autonomous cultural framework" (833). On the basis of a study of narrative practices in two communities in Chicago, one working-class and one middle-class, they concluded that each community had "its own distinct way of structuring children's autonomy" (843). In the working-class community, "in the context of jointly narrated stories of the child's past experiences, children participated freely and thus had extensive speaker rights but were expected to achieve their own authorship by engaging in the practices as a near equal." Narrative autonomy—"to have one's own view and to express it"—emerged as "a prize that young children have to work to obtain." By contrast, the model promoted in the middle-class community proved to be "one where children are given autonomy, in small increments, as a gift from the adults around them": "to express one's views is a natural right, rather than something that has to be earned or defended" (843). As a result, the familiar show-and-tell exercises in U.S. elementary schools, for example, a characteristic forum for practice in self-narration, may prove to be a more comfortable fit for the middle-class child than for the working-class child.[9]

In addition to factors of gender and class, any comprehensive account of the child's achievement of narrative competence needs to include comparative, cross-cultural research. It is a big subject, and I can do no more here than acknowledge its importance. Peggy J. Miller, whose work on the narrative practices of children I find particularly impressive, has this to say about what such investigations should involve: "We need more detailed ethnographic and micro-level description of how various types of discourse are practiced cross-culturally and of how these verbal practices are organized *vis-à-vis* children.... We need to know more about how children participate in and make use of these practices at various ages: what are the conditions under which children acquiesce to, misunderstand, get confused by, playfully transform, or resist socializing messages?" ("Language as a Tool" 88).[10]

Cumulatively, whatever it is that we are acts as a kind of magnet or nucleus attracting particles of life story that we can—and do when prompted—fashion into the forms of life narrative that we recognize as autobiography. By the time we reach adulthood we know how to deliver a suitably edited version of our stories as the occasion requires. For the most part, we are not left to our own devices when we talk about ourselves, for protocols exist for many of the kinds of self-narration we may need to use—in churches,

9. The authors cite research by Michaels.
10. For characteristic examples of Miller's work, see "Instantiating Culture" and "Personal Storytelling."

in courtrooms, in meetings of Alcoholics Anonymous, and so forth. Institutions even produce manuals stipulating the kinds of stories they want us to tell.[11]

I don't think that the process of adult self-narration has attracted anything like the research devoted to the child's practice of "memory talk." Perhaps this is to be expected, for on the face of it we might well ask what more we could learn about an activity so familiar that we perform it without thinking. Yet if we follow the lead of Michel de Certeau, everyday practices of any sort are likely to be rule governed, and self-narration proves to be no exception. This, at any rate, is what Charlotte Linde discovered when she investigated a particular form of "life story," the vocational accounts offered by white middle-class professionals in answer to the question, "What do you do?" Linde concludes that the notion of narrative identity is so deeply rooted in our culture that it functions as a criterion for normality: "In order to exist in the social world with a comfortable sense of being a good, socially proper, and stable person," she comments, "an individual needs to have a coherent, acceptable, and constantly revised life story" (3). Such an expectation is culture specific: as Linde sees it, we happen to live in a culture that subscribes to "the idea that we 'have' a life story, and that any normally competent adult has one." Following the anthropologist Clifford Geertz, she presents narrative identity as "part of the interpretive equipment furnished to us by our culture" (20).

11. See, e.g., Brooks, and Warhol.

What, specifically, does using this equipment require? Above all, the ability to construct a narratively coherent life story. Narrative coherence, Linde argues, derives from principles of causality and continuity, and, once again, it is culture that supplies what she calls "coherence systems," "cultural device[s] for structuring experience into socially sharable narrative" (163). Freudian psychology, Marxism, feminism, most religious faiths—Linde points to these as examples of large-scale sources of narrative coherence. I am struck by the connection Linde makes between narrative self-presentation and normality. She claims that an individual's refusal to supply an appropriate answer to the question "what do you do?" will appear "anomalous and, eventually, sinister" (53). Our performance of self-narration, then, takes place in an environment of social convention and constraint. Having mastered its rules and developed a repertoire of stories about ourselves, we tend—at least socially—to merge with them: in this sense our stories are our selves.

Two caveats: what we think we are, of course, is doubtless not identical to what we say. Moreover, returning to the consequences for the individual of narrative incapacity and memory loss, I would not want to assent to the proposition that the de-storied person has become de-selved. There are many modes of self and self-experience, more than any self-narration or autobiography could relate, and I will conclude this chapter by considering nonnarrative modes of selfhood in the case of an individual suffering from Alzheimer's disease. Nonetheless, in social settings of any kind, it is our narrative identities that define us. So far I have been concerned to establish that when we talk or write about ourselves, there are conventions we need to observe if we want our self-reporting to be accepted by others as satisfactory. Now I want to look more closely at what these rules are and how they work. The stakes turn out to be high, for we are all players in what I have called a narrative identity system, an identity regime that not only sets limits, socially, to what we can say and write about ourselves but determines as well our recognition by others as normally functioning persons.

Narrative Rules, Identity Rules

When we write autobiography or memoir in the United States, our self-reporting may seem to be an expression of the egalitarian individualism enshrined in the Declaration of Independence. May we, though, say and write whatever we please when we engage in self-narration? Not necessarily, as we saw in the James Frey controversy, not unless we are prepared—depending on the nature of the case—to suffer consequences of considerable gravity. A Nobel Peace Prize winner, Rigoberta Menchú, made front-page news when the anthropologist David Stoll accused her of having stretched the truth in her autobiography, prompting journalists to wonder whether the Nobel selection committee would reconsider its prize award to her.[12] The novelist Kathryn Harrison's memoir of her incestuous affair with

12. See Rohter.

her father triggered a flood of condemnation in the press for what was seen as mercenary self-exposure at the expense of her young children.[13] These instances feature published autobiographers, but we are all of us judged when we tell the stories of our lives. This judging, always taking place, manifests itself most strikingly when memory loss and other disabilities prevent our performing self-narration according to the rules, or performing it at all. What all these examples suggest is that while we may well have the right to tell our life stories, we do so under constraints; we are governed by rules, and we can expect to be held accountable to others for breaking them.

As I said before, these rules are tacit because the daily performance of identity story is instinctive and automatic, and so it is chiefly when they are perceived to have been broken that they are most clearly displayed and articulated. I want to consider three primary transgressions—there may be more—for which self-narrators have been called to account: (1) misrepresentation of biographical and historical truth, (2) infringement of the right to privacy, and (3) failure to display normative models of personhood. The seriousness of these charges for those accused is registered in the consequences that may follow from the alleged violations: public condemnation, litigation, and (potentially) institutional confinement. Telling the truth, respecting privacy, displaying normalcy—it is the last of these obligations that points

---

13. For a review of the reception of *The Kiss,* see Eakin, *How Our Lives Become Stories* 153–56.

most directly to the big issue that they all three signal and underwrite: What are the prerequisites in our culture for being a person, for having and telling a life story? To link person and story in this way is to hypothesize that the rules for identity narrative function simultaneously as rules for identity. If narrative is indeed an identity content, then the regulation of narrative carries the possibility of the regulation of identity—a disquieting proposition to contemplate in the context of our culture of individualism. I should note that when I refer to "our culture," I am thinking chiefly of the United States, although one of the examples I will be discussing is drawn from western Europe. My hunch is that wherever self-narration is practiced, it is done under certain tacit constraints; these constraints, however, doubtless vary from culture to culture.

The idea that autobiographical discourse is rule governed is not new, but dates from the dawn of autobiography studies, in the 1970s, when Elizabeth Bruss and Philippe Lejeune established the genre's poetics. Drawing on speech-act theory, Bruss sought to formulate "the constitutive rules" a text needed to satisfy in order to "count as" a bona fide instance of autobiography (8). Similarly, Lejeune highlighted the contractual nature of autobiographical discourse with his notion of a "pact" articulated in the text that determines its generic status for the reader.[14] There is nothing in the least trumped up about this talk of "pacts" and "rules"; to the contrary, Bruss and Lejeune were only bringing system

14. See Lejeune, "The Autobiographical Pact."

and order to the rule consciousness hovering close to the beginning of most autobiographies. For a delicious send-up of the promises and disclaimers that autobiographers instinctively make before they get started, read the elaborate Shandean prefaces to Dave Eggers's *A Heartbreaking Work of Staggering Genius* (2000), or Sterne's *Tristram Shandy* itself. Wallowing in "The Knowingness about the Book's Self-Consciousness Aspect" (xxvi), Eggers produces in effect a playbook for writing memoir by the rules. My primary concern with rules is different from Bruss's, Lejeune's, and Eggers's, however, for I am approaching autobiography not only as a literary genre but also as an integral part of a lifelong process of identity formation. Written autobiographies represent only a small if revealing part of a much larger phenomenon, the self-narration we practice every day. Thus the rules question I want to examine is not only What is expected of this text in order for it to "count as" autobiography? but also What is expected of this individual, as manifested in this self-narration, for him or her to "count as" a person?

Telling the truth—this is surely the most familiar of the rules we associate with autobiographical discourse, and I think that the importance we attach to it is abundantly clear in the James Frey controversy I discussed earlier. Definitions of autobiography as a literary genre inevitably feature truth-telling as a criterion, and Bruss is no exception, for she made truth-value the centerpiece of her analysis of the autobiographical act (10–11). I have been arguing, though, that autobiography's narrative rules also function as identity rules, and that when they do, the rule-defined entity may shift from text to person. When the public responds to rule-breaking autobiographers, not only the literary function of autobiographical discourse but its identity function may come into play. You don't make the front page of the *New York Times* as Menchú did for violating a literary convention—or so I thought until James Frey landed there following his high-profile shaming by Oprah Winfrey. Two controversial autobiographies, one by Menchú and one by Binjamin Wilkomirski, illustrate the primacy of identity issues for the reading public; the reception of these texts confirms that the truth-telling rule doubles as both generic marker and identity requirement.

On the face of it, David Stoll's book-length exposé of *I, Rigoberta Menchú: An Indian Woman in Guatemala* (1999) would seem to contradict my point, for he seems initially concerned to establish whether or not the Menchú text belongs to the literature of fact, a question of genre. Stoll, a theorist and historian of Central American revolutionary movements, seeks to determine whether Menchú's chilling account of the injustices and atrocities inflicted on the Maya by government institutions and the army offers reliable eyewitness testimony. For example, did Menchú see her brother Petrocinio burned alive by army forces in the public square at Chajul? Did she work under exploitative conditions on a coffee plantation on the coast? Not, Stoll argues, if she was a student during those years at a Belgian Catholic boarding school in Guatemala City. Although Stoll does not impugn the large-scale truths of Menchú's story, the suffering of her family and her people at the hands of a repressive regime, he does establish the likelihood that Menchú incorporated the experiences of others into a text that purported to be limited to what she had seen with her own eyes.

In the second half of his book, however, Stoll's first question, Is this text telling the truth? is supplanted by a second, Who is the person telling this narrative and why? In an especially interesting chapter, he reconstructs the making of Menchú's narrative and the role it played in the development of her identity.[15] He portrays Menchú as an impressionable young woman who had witnessed a lot of suffering, although she had been away at school when many of the key events she reports took place on her home ground. He theorizes that she became caught up in a revolutionary movement, the Committee for Campesino Unity, that persuaded her to use her story for the purpose of propaganda, enlisting international support for the embattled guerrillas.

What is instructive about Stoll's response to *I, Rigoberta Menchú* is his ambivalence, which colors the unstable tone of the book, depending on whether he is evaluating a text or judging a person. He is by turns dispassionate and accusatory, and the characterization of Menchú and her narrative changes accordingly: when he tests her story as an eyewitness account, he concludes sternly that some of the time she is lying; when he casts Menchú as a revolutionary propagandist, however, he portrays her much more sympathetically

---

15. The composition of the narrative turns out to have been a rather complex project, probably involving others besides Menchú and her collaborator, Elisabeth Burgos-Debray. See Stoll 177–88.

as a mythmaker who had every reason to tell the story she did to the anthropologist Elisabeth Burgos-Debray in Paris in 1982. Some of the time Stoll invokes the literary function of the truth-telling rule, and some of the time what I am calling its identity function; he has not sorted it out.

At the risk of oversimplifying a rather complex case, I want to set Binjamin Wilkomirski's *Fragments* (1995) alongside *I, Rigoberta Menchú* to illustrate the stakes involved in telling the truth. Like Menchú's *testimonio,* Wilkomirski's narrative invokes the authority of the literature of witness; it purports to be an autobiographical account of a child's experience of the Holocaust. In Riga, at the age of two or three, did Wilkomirski witness the execution of a man who may have been his father? Did a woman who may have been his mother give him a crust of bread at Majdanek? Did he see starving children gnawing the flesh off their fingers? The rarity of the young child's perspective in the literature of the Nazi death camps, together with the shocking contents of the story, made the book an instant sensation; *Fragments* was widely translated and won several literary prizes.

Like Menchú's narrative, Wilkomirski's was attacked as untruthful, notably by the Swiss writer Daniel Ganzfried, who claimed that Wilkomirski was not a Latvian Jew who survived the horrors of Majdanek and Auschwitz but a non-Jewish Swiss native, the son of an unwed mother named Yvonne Grosjean. According to Ganzfried, Wilkomirski spent the war years in a Swiss children's home until he was placed with a Dr. and Mrs. Kurt Dössekker in 1945; he was legally adopted by them in 1947. A number of journalists have corroborated Ganzfried's findings, and in the face of mounting outcry against the book, Wilkomirski's German and American publishers, Suhrkamp Verlag and Schocken Books, both withdrew it from circulation in the fall of 1999. Eva Koralnik, Wilkomirski's literary agent, hired the Swiss historian Stefan Maechler to investigate the case, and Maechler's exhaustive report definitively confirmed Ganzfried's charges.[16]

Both Menchú and Wilkomirski claim to have been eyewitness observers of major and disputed passages of twentieth-century history; and both their narratives have been subjected to rigorous fact-checking and verification. Menchú has emerged from this scrutiny comparatively unscathed, while Wilkomirski has been completely discredited. Why? To be sure, the initial revelations about Menchú were disturbing, and she was clearly on the defensive, engaging in various forms of damage control, publishing a new version of her life story, distancing herself from Elisabeth Burgos-Debray, with whom she collaborated on her first autobiography and so forth. But the outcome was certainly not what high-church right-wingers like Dinesh D'Souza had hoped for: the decanonization of the newest saint in the pantheon of Western civ courses at Stanford University and elsewhere. For one thing, her large-scale facts were accurate even if she was guilty of presenting the testimony of others as her own. For another, her motive for doing so, the creation of

16. I draw on articles by Eskin, Gourevitch, and Lappin in reconstructing Wilkomirski's story.

effective propaganda supporting an oppressed people, seems understandable, legitimate, and even admirable.

Wilkomirski's facts, on the other hand, did not check out; he proved to be an impostor, although commentators have been hard-pressed to decide what to make of this flaky, weepy, moody man: Is he shamelessly opportunistic, or delusional? His motives seem inscrutable at best, reprehensible at worst—reprehensible in that doubts about survivors' testimony have the potential to corrode belief in the Holocaust. While Menchú's career as a human rights activist continues, Wilkomirski's career as a Holocaust victim and self-appointed advocate for child survivors of the camps abruptly ended in dishonor. The British withdrew the *Jewish Quarterly* prize for nonfiction from *Fragments* (Wilkomirski did not return the prize money), and the French apparently asked Wilkomirski to return the plaque they gave him. Meanwhile, Wilkomirski was sued in Zurich for fraud in a class-action suit representing some 12,000 readers.[17] In both these rule-breaking controversies, the autobiographer's character supplanted the accuracy of the text as the primary concern, with the identity function of the truth-telling rule overriding its generic, literary function. This is especially clear in the case of *Fragments:* If the book could not pass muster as autobiography, why not simply repackage it as a novel? Because it is not generic status that is at issue; it is

---

17. Blake Eskin, who covered the Wilkomirski case extensively for the *Forward,* alerted me to these developments in Great Britain, France, and Switzerland.

not the text but the person, and Bruno Grosjean-Dössekker-Wilkomirski's credibility seems to have been destroyed.[18]

To break the second rule constraining the practice of self-narration, respect for the privacy of others, is to suffer damage to one's reputation, as with failing to tell the truth. In both cases, in addition to being tried in the court of public opinion, one may—in France and Switzerland, at any rate—be tried in a court of law.[19] Respecting privacy rights, moreover, may well be at odds with telling the truth, indeed, with telling one's story at all. And because we insist on telling our stories, I suspect that most of us break this rule of privacy almost every day, for, as Philippe Lejeune reminds us, "private life is almost always a co-property" (*Moi aussi* 55, my translation). If autobiography involves inescapably the display of privacy, autobiographers lead perilous lives, morally speaking, whether they like it or not; some of them, however, are well compensated for violating privacy—that is one obvious reason for doing it.

When Kathryn Harrison published *The Kiss* in 1997, her memoir of her affair with her father received many hostile reviews, which approached the book as symptomatic of the

18. Elena Lappin reports that Arthur Samuelson of Schocken Books initially responded rather breezily to the charges against Wilkomirski's text: "It's only a fraud if you call it non-fiction. I would then reissue it, in the fiction category. Maybe it's not true—then he's a better writer!" (49). In the event, Schocken Books republished *Fragments* as an appendix to Stefan Maechler's exposé of Bruno Grosjean's Wilkomirski persona. See Maechler.

19. Lejeune reports two cases—admittedly rare—in which publishers were obliged to cut material deemed to have violated the individual's right to privacy; the reissued texts have white spaces indicating the location of the offending passages. See Lejeune, "L'atteinte publique à la vie privée" 72–73.

ethical failings of the so-called age of memoir. Harrison's story did not place her in the by-now familiar position of the victim of child abuse, a position that is central to the literature of incest—she was a junior in college at the time she began a liaison with her father. In publishing her book, did she become a victim of another kind, a martyr to autobiography's rule of telling the truth? Most of the blurbs and some of the positive reviews, usually by other memoirists, praised Harrison precisely for her honesty and courage in telling her shocking story. Whether or not she was a victim, she was seen by some to have victimized her two young children in making her story public. In a revealing exchange at an Authors Guild forum in New York on April 8, 1997, the reporter Warren St. John characterized Harrison's response to a question concerning "the memoirist's responsibility to his or her family" as "cavalier": "'All's fair in love and war, in this case,' she said." St. John notes that Frank McCourt, also on the panel, took a more conservative stance about his disclosure of sensitive family material in his own memoir, *Angela's Ashes* (1996): "I could not write about my mother and her affair with her cousin until she was dead, because she couldn't live through it." At least one person who initially celebrated Harrison's memoir as "an account of a moral victory" apparently had second thoughts. According to St. John, Robert Coles, identified on the dust jacket as the author of *The Moral Intelligence of Children,* "'recanted' a blurb he provided for [*The Kiss*], saying he had not realized Ms. Harrison had young children of her own who would have to cope with her public revelations" (9).

In Harrison's case, it was not the facts of her story that were in dispute—commentators seemed prepared to accept them at face value—but the act of self-narration itself: Should she have told her story at all? Should respect for the privacy of others have taken precedence over an otherwise commendable allegiance to telling the truth? And did Harrison fail to respect her own privacy in disclosing her story? One of the early reviewers, Cynthia Crossen for the *Wall Street Journal,* said as much when she advised Harrison to follow Crossen's grandmother's standard advice, "Hush up." Harrison claims that an inexorable psychological imperative drove her to write her story, but the authority of that motive was compromised for McCourt, St. John, and a good many other commentators by their sense of baser motives at work. Even more than the predictable promotional activities, which included Harrison's appearance on national television's *Dateline* and *Today* shows, a sensation-grabbing feature on Harrison by her husband, Colin Harrison, in *Vogue* captures the moral ambiguities surrounding *The Kiss.* Exploited or exploiter? In the *Vogue* piece, "Sins of the Father," the husband's account of the psychological necessity that drove his wife to tell her story is paired with a glossy full-page photograph portraying the former incest victim as a disturbingly glamorous fashion plate. Even if she was not guilty of "merchandizing pain," as Warren St. John put it, was she guilty of a still graver flaw in writing and publishing *The Kiss,* a fundamental deficiency in moral culture? Curiously, it may well be that Harrison has been judged more harshly for violating privacy—both others' and her own—than for breaking the incest taboo.

Of the three rules for self-narration I have identified, infractions of the last one—the obligation to display a normative model of personhood—can entail the most serious consequence of the entire set: institutional confinement. "Infraction," I am afraid, does not strike the right note, conjuring up as it does a sense of conscious, deliberate action. By contrast, the transgression I am targeting here, while based on the act of self-narration, is surely involuntary, as opposed to the willfulness involved in distorting the truth or invading privacy. With this last rule, it is not so much a question of what one has done but of what one *is:* one is judged by others to be lacking in the very nature of one's being in a profound and disabling way. This issue of normalcy points up the difficulty of finding a single term to characterize the constraints that govern self-narration as a group. "Conventions" suggests something milder, I think, than "rules," something linked to manners and literary forms, whereas "rules" connects more obviously with the idea of discipline and consequences, so I have opted for "rules." Conventions or rules—my discomfort with terminology reflects the fact that my third "constraint" differs in kind from the first two, and I do not want to ignore that difference. To the contrary, in the discussion that follows I want to shift my perspective from the obligations of those who perform self-narrations to the responsibilities of those who receive and judge those performances: this is where the ethical dimension of a narrative identity system is most strikingly displayed, this is where the potential for the regulation of identity narrative to slide into the regulation of identity is realized.

The most arresting instances of self-narrations that involve a failure to display normalcy have been documented in clinical settings, surfacing for our inspection when observers such as Oliver Sacks and Daniel L. Schacter publish such cases and comment on them. I presented Sacks's portrait of Mr. Thompson, a man suffering from Korsakoff's syndrome, in the opening pages of this chapter, for it displays the identity issue I am concerned with in succinct and arresting fashion. As we saw, memory loss inflicted a devastating blow to his sense of continuous identity, severely limiting his ability to articulate a stable narrative account of himself. Working overtime to supply the identity deficit, Mr. Thompson kept generating new selves and life stories minute by minute, making Sacks wonder whether "there is a *person* remaining" (*The Man Who Mistook* 115) beneath this narrative excess. Sacks himself hesitates to embrace the logic of narrative identity that is at work here, the move to read narrative disorder as an index of identity disorder, but the implication that troubles him in the case is precisely the rule of normalcy I am concerned with. Social accountability conditions us from early childhood to believe that our recognition as persons is to be transacted through the exchange of identity narratives. The verdict of those for whom we perform is virtually axiomatic: no satisfactory narrative (or no narrative at all), no self.

What are the consequences for those affected by this linkage between narrative and identity disorders? Mr. Thompson, for example, was not disciplined in any way as a result of his narrative identity inadequacy. Moreover, as far as

I can make out, the medical profession does not interpret impaired narrative competence specifically as a criterion for diagnosis and institutionalization, although there is abundant evidence of the use of narrative in a broad range of therapies.[20] Nonetheless, Michel Foucault and Roy Porter have explored the disciplinary uses of diagnosis in general in Western culture. Closer to home, G. Thomas Couser points to Susanna Kaysen's best-selling memoir for "documentary evidence … that she was hospitalized as much for nonconformity or rebellion as for mental illness." In Kaysen's case, the title of her narrative, *Girl, Interrupted,* captures her sense of the cost of arrested identity. She reports a therapist's comment that her diagnosis—borderline personality syndrome—is easily applied to "people whose lifestyles bother [those in a position to make diagnoses]" (151). We all know, moreover, that in various societies people inconveniently differing from some mainstream norm have been institutionalized or eliminated. What I am suggesting is the potential punishment confronting those who fail to display an appropriately normal model of narrative identity. This disciplinary possibility is latent in any enforcing of norms.

Stepping back from speculation about enforcement, let's consider the ethical issues that come into play when selfhood is claimed to be diminished or absent in these cases.

---

20. Not only is the practice of making narrative believed to confer a therapeutic benefit but the ability to deliver a coherent self-narrative is often accepted as a sign of (recovered) health and normalcy. See, e.g., Marcus, who argues that Freud implies that "a coherent story is in some manner connected with mental health," and that "illness amounts at least in part to suffering from an incoherent story or an inadequate narrative account of oneself" (92).

I find myself returning again and again to Sacks's accounts of individuals suffering from Korsakoff's syndrome, not only because they represent extreme—and hence revealing—examples of memory loss, but also because Sacks includes his own personal response to the clinical observations he is recording, the fear and threat he feels—and we feel with him—in the face of such calamitous injury to identity. In Sacks's reading, the trajectory of these cases runs as follows: because of brain damage, the patients suffer memory loss, which manifests itself in aberrations of self-narration; as a consequence of this neurological event, these de-storied individuals are deemed to have become de-selved. This loss, which he variously describes as a loss of "life" and "existence" as well as "self," fills Sacks with a "peculiar, uncanny horror" (*The Man Who Mistook* 40); confirming his own response, he writes that people who encounter such individuals "are disquieted, even terrified" (111–12) by them. The hallmark of these damaged identities is a loss of affect; as Sacks puts it, "It is not memory which is the final, 'existential' casualty here ... but some ultimate capacity for feeling which is gone" (114).[21]

How precise may we be in describing these momentous determinations about the quality of an individual's

21. The psychologist Daniel L. Schacter's observations concerning individuals suffering from massive amnesias parallel Sacks's. He portrays "Gene," e.g., as stranded in the present: "And just as his recollections of the past are devastated, he thinks little about the future. It does not occur to him to make plans" (149–50). Again, accompanying the atrophy of the extended self in cases of Korsakoff's syndrome is the loss of affect that troubled Sacks (146). Schacter concludes that individuals afflicted by such memory losses are diminished as persons: "When the past vanishes as the result of amnesia and dementia, so does much of the person" (160).

selfhood? As I have suggested, two leading features of these cases seem to be involved: impaired self-narration and loss of affect. First, the inferences concerning self-narration: obviously there is an implied appeal to a model of normal selfhood, and what can we say for sure about that model? Its structure is that of the extended self, stretching across time, and it is this temporal structure, apparently, sustained by memory, that supplies the armature for the meaning of experience, the content of a "life," of an "existence"—what Sacks refers to as "depth" (*Man* 112). Because the performance of self-narration confirms that identity is in working order, it easily becomes a primary criterion for normalcy. Turning to the unnerving loss of affect that fills witnesses with dismay, I would note that what we have is affect in the observer registering the absence of affect in the observed. That is to say that judgments about damaged selves are not necessarily the result of some easily objectified principles but rather the consequence of affect's agency in the observer.[22] If this is the case, then the ethical issues involved in such judgments become quite complex, and our responsibilities not easily determined.

Lest we distance ourselves too quickly from these admittedly extreme clinical examples, we should remind ourselves that analogous instances of narrative identity disorders have become routine in the age of Alzheimer's disease. Advances in contemporary medicine coupled with a rising standard

---

22. For the role of emotion and feeling in the exercise of rationality, see Damasio, *Descartes' Error.*

of living ensure that an ever-growing number of people we know will outlive themselves, in a sense with which most of us are becoming increasingly familiar. How do we respond to incoherence or memory lapses in the self-accounting of the elderly? "She was not herself today," we say, and our comment offers a fairly mild, forgiving, and potentially hopeful assessment of our forgetful relative; perhaps she will be herself tomorrow—"she's at her best," we add, "in the late morning."[23] But a darker question is lurking in the language we use to describe our sense of the identity situation here: Is she a self anymore?

Clinicians and ethicists have retreated with good reason from such totalizing conclusions, especially in the light of growing knowledge about the manifold registers of self-experience, but the extended self that is the protagonist of self-narration enjoys so central a place in our living that we are conditioned to accept it as the hallmark of functioning identity. When we do so, we accept as well a temporal framework for its story—it lives and dies a *narrative* existence. We deal comfortably and even conventionally with the beginning of our story; it is the ending that gives us trouble. "I was born...," we say, and we haul out the family photo albums if we are lucky enough to have them, papering over the void of the extended self's prehistory, the period that so-called

23. Because I am dealing with *failed* narrative here, the evidence is by definition going to be fragmentary, usually presented—when published—in the matrix of a clinical narrative of some kind. This is why I turn from published texts to anecdotal evidence derived from everyday experience. I believe that we all have such stories to tell about non-stories. Similarly, Schacter observes, "I believe that a science of memory has room for both laboratory and everyday studies" (319, n. 29).

infantile amnesia has erased.[24] Adult amnesias, however, bring us face-to-face with the end of identity's story, the collapse of the extended self when the memory and narrative skills that support it fail. When self-narration stops, does self stop? Should we conclude that when the extended self has perished, it is time to pull the plug? If narrative is indeed a category of experience and not merely a literary form, however, can we be so sure that it is no longer functioning just because we can't observe it in its most familiar verbal manifestations? Moreover, some nonverbal, nonnarrative senses of self doubtless continue to function after extended selfhood has run its course. And while we are interrogating the proposition that self-narration is the sine qua non of identity, we should pause to consider its exclusionary implications for those individuals—many autistics, among others—who never master narrative in the first place.[25] Study of the conventions that enter into our conception of the normal person is a huge subject, and I limit my concern here to the decisive role played by the performance of self-narration in establishing our recognition by others as normal.[26]

I have been arguing that what we say or do about identity narrative carries the potential to transfer and apply to identity; that is, under the regime of social accountability, the regulation of narrative and the monitoring of identity go hand in hand. If this is in fact the case, then other questions

24. See Nelson 157–59 on infantile amnesia.
25. See, e.g., Smith.
26. See Hacking, "Normal People," for a useful introduction to the concept of the normal person.

demand our attention: What are the prerequisites for having an identity in our culture? And does everyone get to have one, and on whose terms? While some aspects of personality are obviously part of our genetic endowment, John Shotter and other developmental psychologists persuade me that in important ways we learn from others to be the persons we say we are. Is there a more fundamental social process than this making of identities? It entails not only consequences for those who break the rules but responsibilities for those who enforce them. In mapping some of the rules governing the self-narrations we are taught to perform as children, telling the truth, respecting privacy, displaying normalcy, I am struck by the fact that moral issues color each of them, leading me to conclude that ethics is the deep subject of autobiographical discourse. "The deep subject of autobiographical discourse"—I first used this phrase in an essay I wrote to introduce a collection of essays called *The Ethics of Life Writing.* At that time, my observation was triggered precisely by thinking about the breakdown of narrative identity. In *The Self in Moral Space: Life Narratives and the Good,* David Parker has confirmed my sense that ethics is central to the practice of life writing. "All autobiographers," he contends, "necessarily define themselves in relation to strongly valued goods" (172).

Earlier I proposed that in an American context the right to write our life stories may seem to be a natural extension of our rights to life, liberty, and the pursuit of happiness. I want to turn now to a thought-provoking essay by James Rachels and William Ruddick in which they make liberty itself a precondition of personhood. Distinguishing between *"being alive"* (a "biological notion") and *"having a life"* (a "notion of biography"), they hold that "only persons have lives" (226, 228). To the person they attribute what I would characterize as a distinctly *autobiographical* consciousness, a set of "self-referring attitudes" that "presuppose a sense of oneself as having an existence spread over past and future time" (227). "Victims of dire poverty, illness, and slavery," they reason, "might retain the capacity for social responses and yet have none of the intentions, plans, and other features of will and action that define a life" (228). If you have to be a person in order to have a life and—I would add—a life story, then conversely, do you have to have a life story in order to be a person? When they specify "a sense of oneself as having an existence spread over past and future time" as a criterion of the person, their thinking dovetails suggestively with the notion of the extended self I have been exploring in this chapter: individuals suffering from Korsakoff's syndrome and Alzheimer's disease, for example, would no longer qualify as persons. Our fear of this "personless," post-identity state is reflected in complex controversies about last wishes and life-support systems. In order to address these existential emergencies, we attempt to fashion legal instruments—living wills, durable powers of attorney, and other forms of so-called advanced directives—in which we state now what our intentions will be when our powers of speech may fail us later on.[27]

27. See, e.g., Grady.

"My Father's Brain"

Thinking about Sacks's Mr. Thompson, I opened this investigation of narrative identity by asking, "What is this man without his story?" We don't really have good answers to this question precisely because we are conditioned to count on others to articulate their identities for us in the stories they tell about themselves. As our population ages, however, adult children, devoted spouses, partners, and friends routinely care for those suffering from various forms of dementia that erase their stories, destroying both memory and the narrative competence that make those stories possible. From the rapidly expanding literature of end-of-life accounts that describe this post-narrative condition, here are two contrasting assessments of its identity consequences. Judge Richard Posner gives this stark evaluation of his mother in her final days: "By the time she died she couldn't speak, she couldn't use her hands, she wasn't human" (MacFarquhar 84). By contrast, John Bayley's report of the novelist Iris Murdoch's descent into Alzheimer's disease suggests that identity may well survive even when its bodily support system has been gravely impaired. Bayley acknowledges the "emptiness" (65) and "absence" (53) of his wife's state; she "has forgotten public language" (127–28), he writes, and she has lost time's "conventional shape and progression" (63). Yet "Iris was Iris" (49), he bravely asserts, and he adds, "One needs very much to feel that the unique individuality of one's spouse has not been lost in the common symptoms of a clinical condition" (49). Is identity an endowment? Or is it something we create as we perform it in narrative, something we stand to lose when words and memories fail us? And do Posner's and Bayley's sharply differing views merely reflect the difference between a tough-minded and a sentimental response to the end of self? With these questions in view, let's consider Jonathan Franzen's essay, "My Father's Brain," an unusually nuanced treatment of the connection between narrative and identity prompted by Franzen's witnessing his father in the grip of Alzheimer's disease.

When Franzen begins to read the neuropathologist's report on the autopsy of his father's brain—"*The brain... weighed 1,255 gm and showed parasagittal atrophy with sulcal widening*" (7, emphasis in original)—the dry, technical language conjures up an image of the brain as "a lump of meat" (10): "I remember translating grams into pounds and pounds into the familiar shrink-wrapped equivalents in a supermarket meat case" (7). As he reconstructs his father's slide into dementia in the pages that follow, Franzen resists reductive medicalization of his father's condition, setting against the story of illness and irreversible disintegration a counterstory of his father's struggle to maintain himself intact. Franzen interprets his initial reluctance to apply the term *Alzheimer's* to his father's state as "a way of protecting the specificity of Earl Franzen from the generality of a nameable condition" (19). How, though, to protect the father, "an intensely private person" (24), from the ravages of a malady that invades the privacy of his inner life, attacking memory and time-consciousness, wiping out the history of his personality?

Researching Alzheimer's, Franzen follows the psychiatrist Barry Reisberg in defining the impact of the disease as an undoing of individuation, as the end of extended selfhood. Franzen's assessment of the unfolding of the disease in his father's case, though, is instructively ambivalent. He seems prepared to accept the writer David Shenk's finding that the special significance of Alzheimer's—as Franzen puts it—is "its slowing down of death": "Shenk likens the disease to a prism that refracts death into a spectrum of its otherwise tightly conjoined parts—death of autonomy, death of memory, death of self-consciousness, death of personality, death of body—and he subscribes to the most common trope of Alzheimer's: that its particular sadness and horror stem from the sufferer's loss of his or her 'self' long before the body dies" (29–30). Yet Franzen qualifies Shenk's interpretation in the remarkable passage that follows:

> This seems mostly right to me. By the time my father's heart stopped, I'd been mourning him for years. And yet, when I consider his story, I wonder whether the various deaths can ever really be so separated, and whether memory and consciousness have such secure title, after all, to the seat of selfhood. I can't stop looking for meaning in the two years that followed his loss of his supposed "self," and I can't stop finding it.
>
> I'm struck, above all, by the apparent persistence of his *will*. (30, emphasis in original)

Displacing the medical story that the autopsy report presumes to tell and revising the analyses of Reisberg and

Shenk, Franzen asserts not only that his ailing father man-
aged to keep some kind of hold on selfhood—beneath or
beyond memory and consciousness—but that he, Jonathan,
needed his father to do so: "I think I was inclined...to persist in seeing him as the same old wholly whole Earl Franzen. I still needed him to be an actor in my story of myself"
(15). Three stories, then: a familiar narrative of illness and
decline (the backstory, as it were, of the autopsy report),
and juxtaposed to it two stories of the will—the father's and
the son's—to maintain the integrity of selfhood. Moreover,
Franzen deliberately makes it impossible to separate these
twin stories of the will: what he is and what his father is are
both bound up in the stories—"his story" and "my story of
myself"—that express their linked identities.

Returning to the nursing home after a disastrous Thanks-
giving reunion with his family—Franzen recalls his father
"listing in his wheelchair like an unstrung marionette, eyes
mad and staring, mouth sagging, glasses smeared with strobe
light and nearly falling off his nose" (28)—Earl Franzen
startles his son with this trenchant comment that conveys
"an awareness of his larger plight and his connection to the
past and future": "'Better not to leave,' he told me in a clear,
strong voice, 'than to have to come back'" (29). Franzen
comments, "He was requesting that he be spared the pain
of being dragged back toward consciousness and memory"
(29). The story that Franzen proceeds to tell, then, is not a
simple, one-way story of collapse but a more complex and
conflicted story of his father's will, both the will to resist and
the will to surrender:

He held himself together longer, I suspect, than it might have seemed he had the neuronal wherewithal to do. Then he collapsed and fell lower than his pathology may have strictly dictated, and he chose to stay low, ninety-nine percent of the time. What he *wanted* (in the early years, to stay clear; in the later years, to let go) was integral to what he *was*. And what *I* want (stories of my father's brain that are not about meat) is integral to what I choose to remember and retell. (31, emphasis in original)

Franzen is candid here when he confesses his own need to remember his father as he does in "My Father's Brain," and he is convincing as well when he argues that his father's capacity to will may well have survived independent of his own need to believe that it had. Franzen detects evidence of his father's will not only in his determination to conceal his mental condition but also in his futile attempts to fight it, "small, covert endeavors not to forget" (31)—Jonathan discovers among his father's papers, for example, little scraps of paper with the names and birth dates of his three sons (registered incorrectly in Jonathan's case). The struggle between the inevitability of the father's disintegration and his attempts to resist it comes to a climax in his death, which Franzen reads as one last exercise of his father's will: "I worried then, worry even now, that I made things harder for him by arriving: that he'd reached the point of being ready to die but was ashamed to perform such a private or disappointing act in front of one of his sons" (35). As Franzen recognizes, dying is, or can be, depending on the case, an existential labor. The father's final act of will is yet one more expression of self: "What he *wanted* . . . was integral to what he *was*."

"My Father's Brain" gives a double answer to the question of the connection between self and story. Yes, there may well have been a "seat of selfhood" in his father's being beyond memory and consciousness and the identity narratives that they enable, there may well have been some dying embers of self flaring up from time to time with stirrings of the will. Franzen certainly persuades us that there was more to his stricken father than an empty shell. When words fail, Franzen recognizes that the body still retains a language of its own. Arriving in the hospital room where his father lies dying, Jonathan notes, "There's no way to know if he recognized my voice, but within minutes of my arrival his blood pressure climbed to 120/90" (35). Without language, without story, however, our access to the others in our lives is tenuous at best—"there's no way to know. . . ." As Franzen tells it, when it comes to other people, the link between self and story is crucial for each of us; story functions as the primary avenue to the self of another person. This is the burden of the essay's closing lines:

> "I see now," [my mother] said, "that when you're dead you're really dead." This was true enough. But, in the slow-motion way of Alzheimer's, my father wasn't much deader now than he'd been two hours or two weeks or two months ago. We'd simply lost the last of the parts out of which we could fashion a living whole. There would be no new memories of him. The only stories we could tell now were the ones we already had. (37–38)

Franzen's instinct to posit a register of selfhood beyond language strikes me as exactly right. For Jonathan, Earl Franzen did remain someone, someone with a will, and his story, moreover, was not lost even if it was lost to him. Franzen's next move, however, placing identity, our distinctive individuality, in opposition to the body, seems to me misguided. Determined to protect "the specificity of Earl Franzen from the generality of a nameable condition," Franzen writes:

> Conditions have symptoms; symptoms point to the organic basis of everything we are. They point to the brain as meat. And, where I ought to recognize that, yes, the brain is meat, I seem instead to maintain a blind spot across which I then interpolate stories that emphasize the more soul-like aspects of the self. (19)

Using "My Father's Brain" to counter the pathologist's autopsy report, Franzen sees himself as defending both self (a dematerialized, "more soul-like" self) and story against the materiality of the body, which, to be sure, had struck his father a grievous blow: "The will to record indelibly, to set down stories in permanent words, seems to me akin to the conviction that we are larger than our biologies" (33). There may well be an existential imperative driving our will to invent and maintain identity narrative; as Franzen suggests, setting down our stories may be a way of facing down our mortality. Given the nature of his father's disease, Jonathan Franzen's focus is understandably on what the body had taken away: "countless sticky-looking globs of 'plaque'" (21) occluding "the same old wholly whole Earl Franzen." What this picture of the body as identity's adversary omits, however, is that identity and identity's story are derived from the body in the first place; we are first and last embodied selves. In this chapter my primary concern has been to investigate the social sources of narrative identity, whereas in the next chapter I will examine its somatic sources. There, drawing on the work of the neurologist Antonio Damasio, I will make a case for "the organic basis of everything we are" by arguing not only that self and story emerge from our lives in and as bodies, but that our extended selves, our narrative identities, may contribute to the well-being of our bodily existence.

CHAPTER 2

AUTOBIOGRAPHICAL CONSCIOUSNESS

Body, Brain, Self, and Narrative

In his flamboyant 1855 preface to *Leaves of Grass,* Walt Whitman promised his readers an astonishing experience: "Read these leaves in the open air every season of every year of your life,...and your very flesh shall be a great poem." Reading a book, done right, could work an amazing process of transubstantiation, bringing author and reader into an intimate, embodied relation: "Camerado, this is no book,/Who touches this touches a man." On the face of it, this is pretty extravagant stuff, yet from the neurobiological perspective on self and narrative that I develop in this chapter, Whitman's overheated description of reading a book may be less fantastical than one might think. As I suggested in chapter 1, there are many reasons to believe that what we are could be said to be a narrative of some kind. There I was considering the social dimension of our narrative identities, emphasizing our lifelong participation in a narrative identity system. Now, inspired by Antonio Damasio's *The Feeling of What Happens: Body and Emotion in the Making of Consciousness* (1999), I will explore the somatic, bodily sources of narrative identity. The linguist Charlotte Linde used interviews as the basis for her inquiry into life story and narrative identity; my own parallel investigation relies chiefly on the I-narratives that find their way into published autobiography. In the wake of my exposure to Damasio's research, I find myself reading autobiography in a new way, not only deepening my understanding of narrative identity but also—surprisingly—confirming the truth of Whitman's startling views about reading. What really happens when we read autobiography?

Antonio Damasio and the "Movie-in-the-Brain"

We all know that whatever else autobiography is, it is almost always an I-narrative of some kind. But what, exactly, does an autobiography's "I" represent? When we write or say "I," the pronoun operates reflexively, referring back to the biographical, historical person who writes or utters it. So far, so good—we already know this. But can we say more? For example, consider Pokey, the spunky child-protagonist of Mary Karr's best-seller, *The Liars' Club: A Memoir* (1995). Here is how her story opens:

My sharpest memory is of a single instant surrounded by dark. I was seven, and our family doctor knelt before me where I sat on a mattress on the bare floor. He wore a yellow golf shirt unbuttoned so that sprouts of hair showed in a V shape on his chest. I had never seen him in anything but a white starched shirt and a gray tie. The change unnerved me. He was pulling at the hem of my favorite nightgown—a pattern of Texas bluebonnets bunched into nosegays tied with ribbon against a field of nappy white cotton. I had tucked my knees under it to make a tent. He could easily have yanked the thing over my head with one motion, but something made him gentle. "Show me the marks," he said. "Come on, now. I won't hurt you."...He held a piece of hem between thumb and forefinger. I wasn't crying and don't remember any pain, but he talked to me in that begging voice he used when he had a long needle hidden behind his back. I liked him but didn't much trust him. The room I shared with my sister was dark, but I didn't fancy hiking my gown up with strangers milling around in the living room.

It took three decades for that instant to unfreeze. Neighbors and family helped me turn that one bright slide into a panorama.... (3–4)

The hair on the doctor's chest, the pattern on the child's nightgown, the air of menace—Karr's account of this inaugural, traumatic memory is vivid, circumstantial, and involving, creating a "you-are-there" effect of immediacy that will be the hallmark of the narrative to follow. But where, exactly, are we located? In a text, in the past, in a mind? The shifting nature of the "I" here, speaking in the present even as it personifies itself in the past, makes this question even harder to answer; Karr's seamless prose spans decades with ease. One thing, however, is certain. The passage establishes the narrative as a work of memory, Karr's probing of "one bright slide," long repressed, to yield in "panorama" a terrifying episode that the rest of her memoir will reconstruct, in which the cowering child witnesses her mother, wielding a butcher knife, collapse into madness. Karr presents her narrative, then, as an attempt to recover the truth of the past. Her commitment to fact is signaled not only by the framing page for the first chapter, which presents a dated photograph of her mother ("Texas, 1961"), but also by the acknowledgments section that precedes the narrative, where Karr stresses the years of "research" she invested pursuing her story's "veracity."

Karr's opening moves in *The Liars' Club* are standard and by-the-book for the start of any autobiography. But despite her assurances of factuality, what—I persist in asking—is the status of the I-character in this identity narrative, and of the I-narrator who tells her story? Surely *The Liars' Club* confirms the truth of William Maxwell's shrewd observation that "in talking about the past we lie with every breath we draw" (27). Even allowing for traumatic imprinting, how much can anyone remember in detail decades later about life at age seven? We have only to consider that Karr devotes the first half of the book to recounting Pokey's adventures in 1961 to recognize that obviously a special kind of fiction is unfolding here in which memory and imagination conspire to reconstruct the truth of the past. This is only to say that we tolerate a huge amount of fiction these days in works we accept nonetheless as somehow factual accounts of their authors' lives; we don't bat an eye.

So much fiction in this memoir. And yet. And yet. We need to reckon with Karr's insistence on the ostensibly factual: the dates, the photographs, the narrator's continuing struggle with her memory and her constant fact-checking with her sister Lecia and her mother. She wants to get it right. So how should we read Pokey and her story? Is she only a character in a story, or does she stand for something more, a reasonably accurate portrait of young Mary Karr that would have a documentary, biographical value of some kind? Certainly the autobiographer reminds us frequently of her commitment to autobiographical truth, but in the last analysis, what seems to count most for her is her memory's report of what she once thought and felt; *this* is the past she seeks to reconstruct, and only she can be the arbiter of its truth. For Karr—and for the autobiographers who interest me the most—the allegiance to truth that is the central, defining characteristic of memoir is less an allegiance to a factual record that biographers and historians could check than an allegiance to remembered consciousness and its unending succession of identity states, an allegiance to the history of one's self. One way or another, all autobiography is about self, yet it is a measure of the difficulty of defining human consciousness that the place of self in autobiographical discourse remains comparatively unexamined. Advances today in brain studies, however, make it worth our while to revisit self, the deep core of autobiography's "I."

So let me begin again and ask, what is the relation between Mary Karr and Pokey, the seven-year-old Mary Karr figure in *The Liars' Club?* The French critic and autobiographer Roland Barthes would have had an easy answer to this question: Pokey—or the protagonist of any autobiography—*and the self for which she stands* are both effects of language, and any relation between them would be necessarily arbitrary and unstable. On the inside cover of Barthes's anti-autobiography, *Roland Barthes by Roland Barthes* (1975), these words appear, playfully inscribed in Barthes's own handwriting: "It must all be considered as if spoken by a character in a novel." Despite the nagging implication of some personal connection between author and text that the facsimile of his handwriting generates, Barthes repeatedly undercuts any autobiographical self-reference that the title might lead us to expect, insisting instead that the I-character in his memoir in no way refers to himself: "I do not say: 'I am going to describe myself' but: 'I am writing a text and I call it R.B.'" At this exemplary postmodern moment of his career, convinced that any identity that "R.B." could possibly refer to is elusive and problematic, lacking as it does any substantial central core, Barthes concludes, "Do I not know that, *in the field of the subject there is no referent?*" (56, emphasis in original).

My own earliest view of self was also language centered, like Barthes's, but different. I tried to steer a middle course between the position that self is an effect of language and a more traditional belief that self is some sort of innate, transcendental endowment, something we are born with, something we somehow just "have." Research into early childhood development persuaded me that self and language, mutually enabling and interdependent, emerge in tandem when children learn to talk.[1] Moreover, developmental psychologists who study how children are initiated into their culture's practices of self-narration confirm this view; they document how children learn from parents and caregivers what it means to say "I" as they begin to tell stories about themselves. I was skeptical, however, that we could push our knowledge of the emergence of self-consciousness beyond this early point when children master language and develop narrative competence. I was convinced that "knowledge of the self is inseparable from the practice of language" (*Fictions in Autobiography* 278). In the light of research in developmental psychology and neurobiology, however, I now see good reason to pursue the origins of self before and beneath language, for work in these fields teaches us that self is plural, and that some modes of self-experience are prelinguistic. As I noted in the preface, in "Five Kinds of Self-Knowledge" the cognitive psychologist Ulric Neisser posits five distinct registers of self-experience, two of which predate the acquisition of language in the child's development and are characterized by direct perception unmediated by reflexive consciousness of any kind. The psychologist and psychoanalyst Daniel N. Stern shares Neisser's belief that some senses of self exist "long prior to self-awareness and language," and he pushes the threshold of self's emergence back to birth, "if not before" (6). If Neisser, Stern, and the developmental psychologists trace the emergence of self to

---

1. See Eakin, *Fictions in Autobiography* 191–98.

a point well *before* language, we might say that the neurologist Antonio Damasio traces it to a point *beneath* language. For Damasio, self is not an effect of language but rather an effect of the neurological structure of the brain. He radically expands the meaning of *self,* suggesting its deep implication in the life of the human organism at every level.

In *The Feeling of What Happens,* Damasio reasons that self must preexist language:

> If language operates for the self and for consciousness in the same way that it operates for everything else, that is, by symbolizing in words and sentences what exists first in a nonverbal form, then there must be a nonverbal self and a nonverbal knowing for which the words 'I' or 'me' or the phrase 'I know' are the appropriate translations, in any language.... The idea that self and consciousness would emerge *after* language, and would be a direct construction of language, is not likely to be correct.... If self and consciousness were born de novo from language, they would constitute the sole instance of words without an underlying concept. (108)[2]

Given these assumptions about language, Barthes's assertion that *"in the field of the subject there is no referent"* would be untenable. Damasio's position is diametrically opposed to it.

---

2. Damasio's formulation here, setting up two clear-cut "before" and "after" positions on the relation between self and language (and indeed on the relation between language and its referents), strikes me as problematic to the extent that it does not allow for the possibility of a dynamic interplay between them. Rodney Needham proposes, for example, that "new inner states" may be created and "distinctively experienced" as "new lexical discriminations are made" (77).

I should pause here to emphasize that in the discussion that follows I will be speculating about self in autobiography on the basis of neurobiological theory that is itself already necessarily speculative. Damasio is careful not to overstate his claims when it comes to wrestling with the nature of consciousness. "I regard the thought of solving *the* consciousness problem with some skepticism. I simply hope," he writes, "that the ideas presented here help with the eventual elucidation of the problem of self from a biological perspective" (12, emphasis in original).

The premise of Damasio's theory of self is "the idea that a sense of self [is] an indispensable part of the conscious mind" (7). Self is a feeling, specifically "a feeling of knowing," "a feeling of what happens." And what does happen? The body responds to its encounters with objects in its environment, and it also responds to its own changing internal states. And *self* is Damasio's name for the feeling of awareness or knowing that these events are taking place. To be conscious is to be endowed with this feeling of knowing that is self; the alternative is a pathological condition, which Damasio dramatizes in the striking case of a man undergoing an epileptic absence seizure: "He was both there and not there, certainly awake, attentive in part, behaving for sure, bodily present but personally unaccounted for, absent without leave.... I had witnessed the razor-sharp transition between a fully conscious mind and a mind deprived of the sense of self" (6–7).

For Damasio, the neurobiology of consciousness, which he refers to as "the movie-in-the-brain," must address two interconnected problems: first, "the problem of understanding how the brain inside the human organism engenders the mental patterns we call ... the images of an object"; and second, "the problem of how, in parallel with engendering mental patterns for an object, the brain also engenders a sense of self in the act of knowing" (9). Pursuing his movie metaphor for the stream of consciousness, Damasio asks, how does the brain generate "the movie-in-the-brain," and how does it generate "the *appearance* of an owner and observer for the movie *within the movie*" (11)? (Damasio's italics prod us to note the mind-bending idea of a moviegoer *inside* the movie he or she is watching—we step into the world of an Escher print as Damasio invites us to contemplate what common sense tells us cannot be true.) Underpinning Damasio's bold attempt to answer these questions is his conviction that "consciousness is not a monolith, at least in humans: it can be separated into simple and complex kinds, and the neurological evidence makes the separation transparent" (16). Damasio identifies two distinct kinds of consciousness and self: (1) a simple level of "core consciousness" and "core self"; and (2) developing from it, a more complex level of "extended consciousness" and "autobiographical self."[3]

Underlying these two modes of consciousness, Damasio traces "the deep roots for the self" (22) to a "*proto-self.*" Emphasizing that "we are *not* conscious of the proto-self," he

3. Damasio compares his "separation of consciousness into at least two levels of phenomena" with Gerald M. Edelman's twofold distinction between "primary" and "higher-order" consciousness (338 n. 10).

defines it as "*a coherent collection of neural patterns which map, moment by moment, the state of the physical structure of the organism in its many dimensions*" (174, emphasis in original). This mapping registers the body's *homeostasis,* "the automatic regulation of temperature, oxygen concentration, or pH" in the body (39–40). In this homeostatic activity recorded in the proto-self Damasio discerns the biological antecedents of the sense of self that is central to his conception of consciousness, "the sense of a single, bounded, living organism bent on maintaining stability to maintain its life" (136). From an evolutionary perspective, self is not some abstract philosophical concept but rather a name for a feeling embedded in the physiological processes necessary for survival. Self, then, for Damasio, is first and last *of* and *about* the body; to speak of the *embodied* self would be redundant, for there is no other.[4]

With the advent of core consciousness, which Damasio characterizes as an "*unvarnished sense of our individual organism in the act of knowing*" (125, emphasis in original), a core self emerges that preexists language and conventional memory. This core self "inheres in the second-order nonverbal account that occurs whenever an object modifies the proto-self" (174). Core consciousness, occurring in a continuous wave of transient pulses, is "the knowledge that materializes when you confront an object, construct a neural pattern for it, and discover automatically that the now-salient image of the object is formed in your perspective, belongs to you, and

4. Damasio cites Kant, Nietzsche, Freud, Merleau-Ponty, and others as precedents for his view that "the body is the basis for the self" (347 n. 4).

that you can even act on it" (126). Individual first-person perspective, ownership, agency—these primary attributes of core consciousness are also key features of the literary form of self, the "I" of autobiographical discourse.

The final and highest level of Damasio's three-tier model of mental reality is extended consciousness and autobiographical self, enabled by the human organism's vast memory capacity. Autobiographical memory permits a constantly updated and revised "aggregate of dispositional records of who we have been physically and of who we have usually been behaviorally, along with records of who we plan to be in the future" (173). It is this store of memories that constitutes identity and personhood, the familiar materials of life story and memoir. While it is true that our experience of life story is emphatically linguistic, Damasio aligns himself with developmental psychologists such as Jerome Kagan who maintain that the emergence of the autobiographical self does not require language, and he speculates that bonobo apes and dogs may well possess autobiographical selves.[5]

I have asserted that all autobiography is about self, and Damasio argues that self is a primary constituent of all conscious experience. Is there a link between self in its literary and in its nonverbal, biological manifestations? I believe that there is, especially if we interpret autobiography as in some sense the expression of what Damasio terms the autobiographical self, and I think that this link takes the form

5. Damasio usefully summarizes his thinking about kinds of self in two schematic, summary tables (174–75).

of a shared activity of representation. I propose to explore this connection in three steps: First, how does the body manifest self? Next, how does Damasio articulate this bodily manifestation of self? And finally, how is self expressed in autobiography?

Damasio's answer to the first question is clear: the body manifests self through feeling. In Damasio's account, the brain is engaged at every level in the mapping and monitoring of the organism's experience, and consciousness allows us to know that this activity is going on, endowing us with "the feeling of what happens." But how can we put into words this feeling of knowing—self—in a way that captures its nonverbal bodily nature? How does Damasio respond to this challenge? Damasio approaches consciousness as the philosopher John R. Searle suggests one should, as "an ordinary biological phenomenon comparable with growth, digestion, or the secretion of bile" ("Mystery" 60). But the difficulties set in right away, for whether or not this neurobiological self—this feeling of knowing generated in the body's brain—is truly ordinary, humans seem to be constituted to regard it as every bit as mysterious and elusive to their attempts to represent it as the older transcendental self that it replaces. The puzzle of consciousness and self is nowhere more evident than in the attempts of Damasio and others proceeding from the same biological assumptions to grapple with what they term the "binding problem," which poses "the question of how different stimulus inputs to different parts of the brain are bound together so as to produce a single, unified experience, for example, of seeing a cat"

(Searle, "Mystery: Part 2" 54). Consciousness seems inevitably to generate a sense of some central, perceiving entity distinct from the experience perceived. Damasio stresses, however, that there is no neurological evidence to support such a distinction, for despite the illusion of unified perception that "binding" miraculously creates, multiple centers of activity in the brain produce it. Continuing the long-term attack on Cartesian dualism that he launched in his earlier book, *Descartes' Error*, Damasio urges that his conception of self has absolutely nothing to do with "the infamous homunculus," the notion that there is a distinct space in the brain occupied by the "knower" function ("the little man"), which "possess[es] the knowledge needed to interpret the images formed in that brain" (189).

Damasio's anti-homunculus stance informs the language he uses to express the experience of knowing that constitutes self; it affects his choice of metaphors and his conception of narrative. I have already mentioned the first of his metaphors, the "movie-in-the-brain." He draws his second metaphor from T. S. Eliot's *Four Quartets:* "you are the music while the music lasts." Both metaphors address perception by refusing any split between perceiver and perceived, and both stress process and duration. Paradoxically, although the feeling of knowing generates a sense of individual perspective, ownership, and agency, the rudiments of what will flower eventually as a sense of bounded identity and personhood, these proto-I-character features of consciousness are to be understood as fused with and not standing free from the life experience of which they are a part. The syntax of autobiographical discourse always posits a subject "I" performing actions: *I* do things, *I* feel and will; *I* remember and plan. By contrast, in the underlying syntax of core consciousness, self resides alike in both subject and predicate. Damasio probes this paradox when he writes of "the *appearance* of an owner and observer for the movie *within the movie*" (11), for "there is no external spectator" (171) for the "movie-in-the-brain." Similarly, repeating Eliot's music metaphor, Damasio writes: "The story contained in the images of core consciousness is not told by some clever homunculus. Nor is the story really told by *you* as a self because the core *you* is only born as the story is told, *within the story itself.* You exist as a mental being when primordial stories are being told, and only then.... You are the music while the music lasts" (191).[6] As Damasio's music and movie metaphors suggest, *self inheres in a narrative of some kind.* Narrative identity, then, the notion that what we are could be said to be a story of some kind, is not merely the product of social convention; it is rooted in our lives in and as bodies.

Damasio's extensive use of narrative as a concept to express the experience of self at the level of core consciousness

6. The neurologist Gerald M. Edelman characterizes perceptual events in the brain in a similar musical metaphor: "Think if you had a hundred thousand wires randomly connecting four string quartet players and that, even though they weren't speaking words, signals were going back and forth in all kinds of hidden ways [as you usually get them by the subtle nonverbal interactions between the players] that make the whole set of sounds a unified ensemble. That's how the maps of the brain work by re-entry." Quoting this comment, Oliver Sacks adds that in Edelman's conception of the brain there is "an orchestra, an ensemble—but without a conductor, an orchestra which makes its own music" ("Making up the Mind" 45).

is at once both familiar and distinctive. Whether it unfolds in movies, in music, in autobiographies, or in the brain, narrative is a temporal form, which "maps what happens over time." But for Damasio, narrative is biological before it is linguistic and literary: it denotes a natural process, the "imagetic representation of sequences of brain events" in prelinguistic, "wordless stories about what happens to an organism immersed in an environment" (189). The brain's narrative, moreover, is not only wordless but *untold,* as Damasio's paradoxical movie and music metaphors are designed to illustrate; instead of a teller, there is only—and persistently—what we might call a teller-effect, a self that emerges and lives its life only within the narrative matrix of consciousness. For Damasio, self and narrative are so intimately linked that to speak of the one is reciprocally to speak of the other; I believe that the same holds true for autobiography—hence my growing preference for terms such as *I-narrative, self-experience,* and *identity narrative.*

If my hypothesis is correct, that there is a connection between Damasio's wordless narrative of core consciousness and the expression of self in autobiographical narrative, what are the key points of likeness between these two orders of narrative?

- *They are both temporal forms:* self is not an entity but a state of feeling, an integral part of the process of consciousness unfolding over time.
- *They both generate the illusion of a teller:* although the experience of selfhood inevitably creates a sense that it

is being witnessed or narrated, a freestanding observer/ teller figure cannot be extrapolated from it.

o   *They both serve a homeostatic goal:* the adaptive purpose of self-narrative, whether neurobiological or literary, would be the maintenance of stability in the human individual through the creation of a sense of identity; as self-narration maps and monitors the succession of body or identity states, it engenders "the notion of a bounded, single individual that changes ever so gently across time but, somehow, seems to stay the same" (134).

While I am deeply attracted to the idea that autobiographical narrative might be tied to the well-being of the human organism, an idea that I will explore further in chapter 4, it is the second point, concerning what I have termed the teller-effect, that has more immediate potential not only to illuminate our reading of autobiography but also to enlarge our understanding of the I-characters and I-narrators that structure our stories of our selves.

We tend instinctively to think of autobiography as a narrative container or envelope of some kind in which we express our sense of identity, as though identity and narrative were somehow separable, whereas Damasio's account of self posits that our sense of identity is itself generated *as* and *in* a narrative dimension of consciousness.[7] Recall Damasio's

7. Like Frank Kermode in *The Sense of an Ending,* Damasio stresses narrative as much more than a literary form, approaching it instead as a sense-making structure that maps and monitors temporal events. I should emphasize that in drawing attention to the movie and music metaphors Damasio uses to develop his thinking—the apparently paradoxical notion, for example, of a "wordless"

"movie-in-the-brain" figure, which nicely encapsulates the gulf between experiential and neurological accounts of consciousness. We all can testify that consciousness generates "the *appearance* of an owner and observer for the movie" unfolding in our heads, while neurological findings oblige Damasio to stress that the owner-observer figure is located—paradoxically—"*within the movie*" it seems to witness and not outside it. Our sense of having selves distinct from our stories is, nevertheless, hugely productive, serving our need for a stable sense of continuous identity stretching over time. When we talk about ourselves, and even more when we fashion an I-character in an autobiography, we give a degree of permanence and narrative solidity—or "body," we might say—to otherwise evanescent states of identity feeling. We get the satisfaction of seeming to see ourselves see, of seeming to see our selves. That is the psychological gratification of autobiography's reflexiveness, of its illusive teller-effect.

To recognize the teller-effect as an illusion, however, to understand selfhood as a kind of "music" that we perform as we live, can prompt us to locate the content of self-experience in an autobiography not merely in the central figures of the I-character and the I-narrator, where we are conditioned to look for it, but in the identity narrative as a

---

or untold story—I do not mean to imply that there is anything loose or merely metaphorical about the concept of narrative these figures are intended to express. For further discussion of the proposition that narrative could be said to be a mode of consciousness rooted in phenomenological experience, see Eakin, *Touching the World* 190–98.

whole. Returning to *The Liars' Club,* then, it would be the I-narrative *about* Pokey and not just the Pokey-character it features that would be the true locus of Mary Karr's reconstruction of her earlier self.[8] If, in the counterintuitive syntax of consciousness, self inhabits both subject and predicate, narrative as well as character, then autobiography not only delivers metaphors of self, it *is* a metaphor of self. The narrative activity in and of autobiography is an identity activity. Borrowing Damasio's borrowing of T. S. Eliot's metaphor, we might say that *The Liars' Club is* Mary Karr while she writes her story and perhaps even while we read it too: she *is* the music of her narrative while the music lasts. Why does she need to get her story straight? Not just to satisfy the biography police but to respond to a psychological imperative that gravitates to the performance of narrative as integral to the experience of identity. Narrative is the name of the identity game in autobiography just as it is in consciousness and in interpersonal relations (as we saw in chapter 1), and nowhere more so than in *The Liars' Club,* where Karr makes clear that her own practice of self-narration is rooted in her father's tall-tale telling, which shaped her childhood and her artistic vocation. If her childhood is filled with stories, so is her adult life, in which, she tells us, the narrative work of psychoanalysis played into the writing of her autobiography.

8. In identifying Pokey as the I-character in *The Liars' Club,* I am simplifying a rhetorical situation of considerable complexity in which the distinction between protagonist and narrator is fluid, for protagonists often assume, as Karr's does, a narrator function, and narrators cumulatively take on the solidity of a character.

And the autobiography's account of all this making of identity narrative comes to a climax and closure with the twin
stories-within-stories of her father's final tale and her mother's confessional revelations about her hidden past, a past so
wounding that it had driven her to the knife-wielding act of
madness that opens the memoir. Nowhere is Karr's belief in
narrative as the motor of identity more strikingly displayed
than in her response to her father's stroke at the end of the
book. Devastated by the blow that silences Pete Karr and
his voice for good, she responds to his aphasia by playing
for them both a tape of one of his tall tales—and, we might
add, by writing *The Liars' Club*.[9] When we write autobiography and when we read it, we repeat in our imaginations the
rhythms of identity experience that autobiographical narratives describe. I believe that the identity narrative impulse
that autobiographies express is the same that we respond to
every day in talking about ourselves; both may be grounded
in the neurobiological rhythms of consciousness.

Doing Consciousness

I began this inquiry into narrative identity by pointing to
the process of self-narration constantly unfolding in our

---

9. Karr makes clear that the tape functions simultaneously as the record of
a story and the record of an identity: "I started shuffling through a shoebox of
cassette tapes on the floor till I laid hold to the one with 'Pete Karr' on the label in
red Magic Marker" (303).

heads. Doesn't Antonio Damasio's neurobiological perspective on self and narrative, however, unsettle this familiar experience? What becomes of the central player who animates our stream of consciousness, this "I" who thinks and feels and plans, if it can be properly described as merely a "teller-effect"? How can a "teller-effect" be endowed with a capacity for action? If we are to fathom this sense of a disconnect between the reality of our experience on the one hand and what neurobiological research can teach us about it on the other, we need to distinguish carefully between levels of analysis. Whereas, neurologically speaking, the structures that support selfhood are distributed across many areas in the brain, from a phenomenological perspective, the experience of selfhood is indeed centered, and is certainly the locus of conscious intentions; a neurological "effect" is nonetheless and simultaneously a profound experiential reality. When we visit the interface between levels of reality, each with competing truth claims, how, then, should we respond? This is precisely the issue that George Lakoff and Mark Johnson address in *Philosophy in the Flesh* (1999), when "a scientific truth claim based on knowledge about the neural level is contradicting a truth claim at the phenomenological level" (105). "The phenomenological and neural levels," they remind us, "provide different modes of understanding, the first in terms of everyday experience and the second in scientific terms" (106). And so they ask, "do we want to say that only one of these levels is relevant to explanation?" (108). "Embodied truth," they conclude, "requires us to give up the illusion that there exists a unique correct description of any situation. Because of the multiple levels of our embodiment, there is no one level at which one can express all the truths we can know about a given subject matter" (109).

Does neurobiological knowledge have the power, then, to undermine the truth of our experience of selfhood? No one, I think, has anything to fear from Damasio's account of consciousness on the score of agency. In fact, I would say that the psychologist Daniel M. Wegner's *The Illusion of Conscious Will* (2002), which also brings to bear a neurobiological perspective on mental activity, presents a much more formidable challenge to belief in our capacity to will our actions. I certainly thought so when I read the column by John Horgan in the *New York Times* that brought Wegner's work to my attention. I was working on the ethics of life writing at the time, so I was primed to wonder what might become of morality, of personal responsibility, if conscious will proved indeed to be an illusion. According to Wegner, the findings of brain studies are at odds with what we think we know about our actions: "*The experience of consciously willing an action is not a direct indication that the conscious thought has caused the action*" (2, emphasis in original). Instead, "the experience of conscious will kicks in at some point *after* the brain has already started preparing for the action" (54, emphasis in original). Because "we can't possibly know (let alone keep track of) the tremendous number of mechanical influences on our behavior...., we develop a shorthand, a belief in the causal efficacy of our conscious thoughts" (27–28). What is the relation between our representation of conscious experience—whether of the will or of self—and the totality of mental life both conscious and unconscious that our representations purport to describe? Wegner's notion of a shorthand that we employ to make sense of our experience strikes me as apt, and not disabling when it comes to ethics, for we operate as intending moral human beings on the basis of our apprehension of conscious experience and not from a conceptual knowledge of its neurobiological substrate.

But what if brain damage limits our ability to function as purposeful moral agents? Recent developments in neuroscience have been invoked to challenge traditional conceptions of moral responsibility. Neuroscientific findings, notably in the form of brain scans, have been introduced in American courts as a defense against criminal charges.[10] In *The Ethical Brain,* the cognitive scientist Michael Gazzaniga captures the potential reductiveness of such neurobiological accounts of human conduct in a witty chapter title, "My Brain Made Me Do It." What such explanations omit, he argues, is the world of social and cultural experience that shapes the values we acknowledge as guiding our actions. When it comes to responsibility, Gazzaniga stresses the distinction between the physiological and social dimensions of our experience: "Brains are automatic, rule-governed, determined devices, while people are personally responsible agents, free to make

10. The ethical and legal implications of such evidence are extremely complex and only beginning to be investigated by experts in the emergent fields of neuroethics and neurolaw. For a brief overview of some of the key issues, see Rosen.

their own decisions" (90). Despite this caution about the gap between neural and social registers of experience, Gazzaniga proposes to negotiate it when he advocates a search for a "universal ethics" that would take the embodied nature of our humanity into account. "Knowing that morals are contextual and social, and based on neural mechanisms," he urges, "can help us determine certain ways to deal with ethical issues" (177). It is precisely the idea that morals have a basis in neural mechanisms, though, that has seemed to cloud the familiar precept of taking responsibility for our actions. What if those mechanisms become impaired or never function properly in the first place? The journalist Malcolm Gladwell describes research by the psychiatrist Dorothy Lewis and the neurologist Jonathan Pincus into the organic causes of criminal violence. Their work, which targets the link between ethics and the brain, suggests that brain injuries (notably frontal-lobe damage) combined with childhood abuse can produce "such terrifying synergy as to impede…individuals' ability to play by the rules of society" (Gladwell 135). The etiology of violence that Lewis and Pincus reconstruct leads Gladwell to conclude, "Advances in the understanding of human behavior are necessarily corrosive of the idea of free will" (145–46), indeed "corrosive of self" (142). "Is a moral standard still a moral standard," Gladwell asks, "when it is freighted with exceptions and exemptions and physiological equivocation?" (147).

When I read about the thought-provoking research of Wegner, Lewis, Pincus, and others, it can seem as though we are being asked, in the name of cognitive science, to exchange a sublimely clear picture of cause and effect on the order of Michelangelo's Sistine ceiling for a mass of firing neurons. Should it make us uneasy, then, to think that what we are as individuals, as selves, as persons, is derived from our human nature as biological organisms? Antonio Damasio celebrates what the brain creates, while Lewis and Pincus remind us of what the brain can destroy; what the body gives us—self and the moral life—it can also take away. As Jonathan Franzen, faithful witness to his father's inexorable mental decline, put it in "My Father's Brain," surely "we are larger than our biologies" (33), yet he also acknowledges "the organic basis of everything we are" (19). And where does that acknowledgment take us when it comes to selfhood? The cognitive scientists Gerald M. Edelman and Giulio Tononi capture the aim of my investigation of Mary Karr's autobiography in this memorable formulation of their own research: "We are trying to connect a description of something out there— the brain—with something in here—an experience, our own individual experience, that is occurring to us as conscious observers" (11). Consider the representation of self, I proposed, in a passage from Mary Karr's memoir, juxtaposing two different perspectives, one literary and one neurobiological. This modest experiment taught me two things: (1) that "self" content might be distributed throughout an I-narrative and not merely contained in the I-characters and I-narrators where the conventions of autobiographical discourse condition us to look for it; and (2) that "self" is not only reported but performed, certainly by the autobiographer as she writes and perhaps to a surprising degree by the reader as he reads. As far as our capacity for action is concerned, I saw more self, more agency, than I had before, not less. As Antonio Damasio might have put it, in writing autobiography Mary Karr was doing self, doing consciousness: "You are the music while the music lasts."

"Doing consciousness"—this emphasis on autobiography as performance, as action, will be my theme in the rest of this book. In the first two chapters I have sketched out the social and somatic "givens" of our narrative identities, the factors that temper the illusion of total autonomy inevitably accompanying our acts of self-presentation—those moments when *we* say who we are. But indeed we *do* say who we are, and in the final chapters of this book I want to look at how particular individuals use the cultural and somatic equipment they are given when they make identity narrative. In chapter 3, resuming the social perspective that guided my inquiry in chapter 1, I attempt to discriminate the part of freedom in the mix of cultural and specifically economic forces that govern the identity work society requires of us as players in a narrative identity system. In chapter 4, by contrast, picking up on my concerns in chapter 2, my perspective is at once narrower, targeting the body's homeostatic requirements, and much, much broader, proposing that the act of autobiographical self-fashioning that we perform every day may possess an adaptive, evolutionary value for the human organisms that we are. The materials I am working with in these chapters—published autobiographical narratives—are literary, to be sure, but as I see it, they are much more than that, offering a precious because tangible record of an otherwise evanescent process of identity construction that is central to our lives. It is this existential imperative in our talking and writing about ourselves that I seek to recognize when I speak of these acts as "living autobiographically."

CHAPTER 3

IDENTITY WORK

People Making Stories

In the winter of 1849–50, at work on his ambitious project to chronicle the lives of London's working poor, Henry Mayhew interviewed an eight-year-old girl selling watercress in the streets of the East End. "The poor child," he writes, "although the weather was severe, was dressed in a thin cotton gown, with a threadbare shawl wrapped round her shoulders. She wore no covering to her head, and the long rusty hair stood out in all directions." The child's account of herself opens as follows:

"I go about the streets with water-creases, crying, 'Four bunches a penny, water-creases.' I am just eight years old—that's all, and I've a big sister, and a brother and a sister younger than I am. On and off, I've been very near a twelvemonth in the streets. Before that, I had to take care of a baby for my aunt. No, it wasn't heavy—it was only two months old; but I minded it for ever such a time—till it could walk.... Before I had the baby, I used to help mother, who was in the fur trade; and, if there was any slits in the fur, I'd sew them up. My mother learned me to needle-work and to knit when I was about five. I used to go to school, too; but I wasn't there long. I've forgot all about it now, it's such a time ago...." (1:151)

The historian Carolyn Steedman, drawing on her own research into the lives of working-class girls to examine this child's bleak story, claims that such children learn at an early age to know their places in an economic system. The child's sense of identity, she observes, was informed by a stark "economic vision" (*Landscape for a Good Woman* 135): "Her labour functioned as a description of herself—or rather, she used it as a description of what she knew herself to be...a worker, a good and helpful little girl, a source of income. *In this situation her labour was not an attribute, nor a possession, but herself;* that which she exchanged daily for the means of livelihood, for love, and food and protection" (*Landscape* 136, emphasis added).[1] Thinking about Mayhew's little watercress seller and Steedman's comments, I find myself wondering whether determinism—in this case economic—lurks at the heart of our identities, identities that we characteristically associate with values of freedom

---

1. For nineteenth-century working-class children's sense of "economic self-hood," see Steedman, *The Tidy House* 110–31.

and autonomy. To what extent are the selves we think we are and the life stories we think we've lived the product of our position in a field of large-scale cultural forces? Look again at Steedman's analysis of the little watercress seller. The terrain is slippery here, as Steedman's ambivalent formulation suggests: the child is equivalent to her work ("*her labour was…herself*"), or, alternatively, the child "uses" her work to articulate "what she knew herself to be." How to discriminate agency from conditioning in this matter of identity? As Steedman's nuanced account of the child's sense of self implies, and as I mean to show in the discussion that follows, we never experience the cultural forces in our lives in a simple and transparent way. In previous chapters I have considered both the social and somatic sources of narrative identity, and it is certainly true that these givens of our experience can seem to entail a rather limiting estimate of the possibility of self-determination in human culture. With this shadow of determinism in view, I want first to consider the model of individualism that underwrites narrative identity and its representation in Western life writing, and then to evaluate narrative identity as a practice. It is not easy to assess the impact of individualism on our thinking about our selves and lives, for such a belief tends to promote a false sense of empowerment, masking the work of the other forces that shape us. While our narrative self-fashioning is certainly constrained (extremely so in the case of Mayhew's little watercress seller), I conclude nonetheless that *we* perform it according to our lights; we get the good of saying and writing who we are.

Looking at Vermeer: "Inner" Lives and "Outer" Forces

I have always been fascinated by Vermeer, so when professional travel took me to Germany I seized the chance to see the Vermeer in Frankfurt with a friend. We were not disappointed as we stood gazing at *The Geographer*. In Paris, as a youth, I had seen the companion painting, *The Astronomer*, and now, a lifetime later, I saw its twin. After looking long at *The Geographer* in silence, my friend and I began to talk about it. Critics and teachers ourselves, how could we help but be drawn to this portrait of an individual lost in thought? There is a spellbinding sense of arrested movement in the geographer's posture, the dividers or compass poised in his hand, his abstracted gaze; he is not looking at anything material before him, although he is surrounded by the maps, globe, and related instruments of his calling. I told my friend that I had attended a conference earlier in the summer where I had heard a historian assert that there was no such thing as an inner self in Western culture before the end of the eighteenth century. According to this speaker, any attempt to locate evidence of interiority as we know it in an earlier period would be an irresponsible, ahistorical move. Looking at *The Geographer* and the other Vermeers I have seen, however, I remain irresponsibly convinced that the culture of individualism that informs our own narrative identity system was already in play in the time of Vermeer and his contemporaries.

In fact, while cultural historians concur in affirming the existence of a distinctive kind of selfhood in the modern period, they assign various dates to its emergence—anywhere from 1500 to 1800. Karl J. Weintraub, for example, assumes that this emergence had already taken place by the end of the eighteenth century, and he attributes the rise of Western autobiography at this time in the work of Rousseau and Wordsworth to two key developments: "the recognition of a strong historical dimension of all human reality" and "a modern mode of self-conception as an individuality" (847). In the light of studies by Philippe Ariès, Lionel Trilling, Lawrence Stone, and Charles Taylor, I speculated in 1992 that this new attention to life story and individuality was linked to the rise of bourgeois capitalism. "Modern autobiography," I wrote, "seems to have emerged concurrently with—and is perhaps a symbolic manifestation of—people's acquisition of a distinctly personal space in which to live, rooms of their own, in which, according to architect Witold Rybczynski, the bourgeois values of privacy, intimacy, and 'home' could flower" (*Touching the World* 100–1). At the time I was very much under the spell of Rybczynski's *Home: A Short History of an Idea* (1986), in which he argues that shifts in the design of domestic space in places like seventeenth-century Protestant Holland led to "the emergence of something new in the human consciousness: the appearance of the internal world of the individual, of the self, and of the family" (35).

So what did this new "internal world of the individual" look like in the seventeenth century? A decade later, a splendid small exhibition, "Love Letters: Dutch Genre Paintings in the Age of Vermeer," which I saw at the Bruce Museum in Greenwich, Connecticut, seemed to provide me with the answer. The paintings in the show by Vermeer, Pieter de Hooch, and Gerard ter Borch portrayed well-dressed individuals captured in the act of writing or reading letters. These people had the education, leisure, and private space in which to set down their thoughts, and those thoughts, in turn, seemed almost visible, acquiring a kind of immediacy and value by virtue of their association with the wonderfully rendered material objects of the letters themselves. You felt that you could almost touch the letters—in many cases it was possible to make out the writing—never has paper looked so good. In these pictures of seventeenth-century letter writers and readers, the Dutch masters made self-expression the focal point of gleaming interiors, thoughts and feelings honored by their association with such handsome things. I felt sure that the inner lives of these people were being celebrated, but were they also being treated as things? It is hard to be sure, for the paintings were destined for show in affluent settings very like the ones they displayed.

However one reads it, the connection Rybczynski articulates between consciousness and domestic space, a connection ultimately between person and property, is one that has been a constant in thinking about individualism from the seventeenth century to the present day. In the early modern period, for example, according to C. B. Macpherson, European political theory from Thomas Hobbes to John Locke featured "possessive individualism," which posited the individual "as an owner of himself" (3). Two centuries later, in the United States, Samuel D. Warren and Louis D. Brandeis made a similar link between person and property when they based their concept of the individual's right to privacy and hence the right to "an inviolable personality" on "the right of property in its widest sense" (85). They sought legal recognition of the individual's right "to be let alone," a phrase they borrowed from Justice Thomas Cooley of the Michigan Supreme Court, who had used it in 1888 in connection with a case concerning liability for assault. In the years following Warren and Brandeis's landmark 1890 article on "The Right to Privacy," the association of person with property continued. Surveying privacy cases in the United States up to 1960, William Prosser identified four distinct torts: (1) "intrusion upon the plaintiff's seclusion or solitude, or into his private affairs"; (2) "public disclosure of embarrassing private facts about the plaintiff"; (3) "publicity which places the plaintiff in a false light in the public eye"; and (4) "appropriation, for the defendant's advantage, of the plaintiff's name or likeness" (107). Only the first tort, with its reference to "solitude," invokes a notion of an "inviolable" interiority; the rest target dissemination of information in print or image.

Do we, then, own our selves and the stories of our lives? Privacy, property—is it capitalism that accounts for the potentially jarring linkage of inner states to material possessions, a connection that crossed my mind as I looked at the Ter Borchs, Vermeers, and De Hoochs? Judge Richard A. Posner's economic theory of privacy, for instance, pits privacy and prying against each other as two competing "economic goods" in a world where—he claims—"few people want to be let alone" (338). One might well think otherwise, for current debates—about a woman's right to choose, for example, or a terminally ill patient's right to die—suggest that many Americans believe that the right to privacy and the individual's liberty it supports are threatened. Economic prosperity may have generated the possibility of rooms of one's own, and selves and lives to lead in them, as Rybczynski proposes, but in the present age in which personalities are marketed as commodities—you can buy *People* at the supermarket checkout—modern individuality may be under attack. The demand for personal information and the technology that makes it easy to get are hard to withstand; now more than ever, it may be hard "to be let alone."

Technology was already an issue for Brandeis and Warren in 1890. They argued that "recent inventions and business methods" had created the need for a new kind of legal protection of the person that their concept of a right to privacy was meant to secure: "Instantaneous photographs and newspaper enterprise have invaded the sacred precincts of private and domestic life; and numerous mechanical devices threaten to make good the prediction that 'what is whispered in the closet shall be proclaimed from the house-tops'" (76). Now, a century later, new technologies are again altering the conditions under which selves can be displayed and privacy maintained. The Internet and the World Wide Web are creating radically new opportunities for self-presentation, and perhaps, some observers think, new modes of selfhood as well. Jeffrey Wallen's investigation of online journals or weblogs, for example, leads him to speculate that "the contemporary 'self' is in important ways discontinuous with what existed at earlier times." His findings parallel those of the French autobiography critic Philippe Lejeune, whom he quotes as follows: "The self [*moi*] is not an atemporal essence altered today by disastrous technical progress,…it has always been shaped by the evolution of medias" (Lejeune, *Cher écran* 240).

It is certainly true that the speed and ease of logging on seem to be rapidly changing the nature of social interaction for those who have come of age with the advent of computer technology—where in the world today are there not Internet cafés? In his profile of the "me media" Facebook and MySpace, John Cassidy cites research by the Pew Internet & American Life Project documenting that "eighty-seven per cent of Americans between twelve and seventeen years old are online, and more than half of them have created some form of digital content and uploaded it to the Internet: a home page, a blog, a photo album, or a video clip" (55). Predictably, the social world of cyberspace seems to have developed its own version of the rule-governed narrative identity system I described in chapter 1. As Chris Hughes, a Facebook founder, puts it, "If you don't have a Facebook profile, you don't have an online identity" (56). When it comes to the issue of access to personal information, dating and other online encounter services might seem to confirm the truth of Posner's claim that "few want to be let alone." But the managers of the social-networking sites interviewed by Cassidy tell a different story. "People want access to all the information around them," comments Facebook co-creator Mark Zuckerberg, "but they also want complete control over their own information" (54). Facebook's solution to this dilemma is to give its users the option of limiting access to their personal sites. The endless ingenuity of hackers, however, makes me wonder whether control over one's online identity isn't wishful thinking. Despite the aura of self-determination (as in "self-made man") that we associate with individualism, does this model of the person obscure the extent to which people in the modern state—both online and off—are subject in the very core of their identities to economic, social, and political pressures beyond their control?

The anthropologist Marianne Gullestad, for example, claims that "global capitalist modernity has put autobiography, morality, and self-fashioning into the foreground in new and forceful ways."[2] Studying life stories has led her to conclude that individualism in Western societies is not only an opportunity but a burden:

> Modern secular society puts increasing pressure on individuals by investing the individual self with profound importance and making each person solely responsible for the development of his or her own self, on the one hand, and, on the other hand, by divorcing the individual from forms of communities which give that development direction and meaning. The individual self is thus remarkably precarious and remarkably important. (287–88)

---

2. *Everyday Life Philosophers* 10. Unless otherwise noted, all references to Gullestad are to this text.

To test the truth of such an observation, we need to bridge the gap Gullestad posits between "the ways in which ideal life courses and identity categories are constructed by the state, the market, and the mass media, on the one hand" and "how people in their everyday lives construct themselves as subjects, on the other" (306).

If we accept Gullestad's assertion that there is a connection between globalization and individualism, it then becomes a challenge to understand how identity formation unfolds as part of a larger, informing economic structure and the cultural processes it sets in motion. For one instructive formulation, consider the philosopher Ian Hacking on the emergence of the "meta-concept" of normality, which he identifies as "one of the most understudied phenomena of the industrial and information-theoretic worlds in which we lived and live." Hacking asserts that the Industrial Revolution ushered in a paradigm shift in the Western concept of the person: "During the nineteenth century, the idea of normal people displaced the Enlightenment ideal of Human Nature" ("Normal People" 59). Citing what Michel Foucault calls the constitution of subjects, Hacking directs our attention to the curious phenomenon of "making up people": "Social change creates new categories of people, . . . new ways for people to be. People spontaneously come to fit their categories" ("Making Up People" 223). In this view, models of the person are culture specific and period specific; there is always a dynamic interplay between particular individuals and the available descriptions for kinds of human beings. By way of illustration, Hacking points to the multiple personality as a new category of the person that emerged in the last part of the nineteenth century: "I claim that multiple personality as an idea and as a clinical phenomenon was invented around 1875: only one or two possible cases per generation had been recorded before that time, but a whole flock of them came after" ("Making Up People" 223). Bureaucrats, statisticians, and social observers of various kinds create categories of persons; individuals in their everyday lives embody categories. Hacking proposes the notion of a feedback loop to describe this process of classification and embodiment in action: "New sorting and theorizing induces changes in self-conception and in behaviour of the people classified. Those changes demand revisions of the classification and theories, the causal connections, and the expectations. Kinds are modified, revised classifications are formed, and the classified change again, loop upon loop" ("Looping Effects" 370).

Thinking about the interplay between theorists and ordinary citizens in this matter of identity categories, I find myself recalling the work of the great twentieth-century sociologist David Riesman, who believed that models of identity in a culture emerge in response to large-scale social forces. In *The Lonely Crowd* (1950) Riesman presents a vision of a United States undergoing unprecedented social change in the years following the Second World War, a change manifested in a major shift in national "character" types from the "inner-directed" model that earlier generations of Americans had internalized to a new "other-directed" model of the person. "Inner-directed" for Riesman means that "*the source of direction for the individual is 'inner' in the sense that it is implanted early in life by the elders and directed toward generalized but nonetheless inescapably destined goals"* (15, emphasis in original). *"What is common to all other-directeds,"* by contrast, *"is that their contemporaries are the source of direction for the individual—either those known to him or those with whom he is indirectly acquainted, through friends and through the mass media"* (22, emphasis in original). What interests me in Riesman's analysis is the correlation he makes between particular character types and population phases in modern Western history (14, 26). Riesman charts the emergence of the inner-directed individual from the Renaissance onward as the dominant character type in the West, against the backdrop of a society "characterized by increased personal mobility, by a rapid accumulation of capital (teamed with devastating technological shifts), and by an almost constant *expansion:* intensive expansion in the production of goods and people, and extensive expansion in exploration, colonization, and imperialism" (15, emphasis in original). For Riesman, then, economic pressures play no small part in configuring social structure and the models of character that individuals internalize in the work of self-fashioning. While Riesman himself displayed a keen awareness of the potential for reductiveness in the character categories he deployed in *The Lonely Crowd* (6–7), they certainly achieved a wide currency in the 1950s. When people I knew in those years described someone as "other-directed," for example, they were invoking precisely the kind of labeling, of modeling of the person, that Hacking sees as part of the endless spooling of identity categories in response to social change.

When David Riesman traces the emergence of character types to population phases, when Ian Hacking associates shifts in the concept of the person with the Industrial Revolution, when Marianne Gullestad connects individualism and globalization, I think they are making very large claims about how models of self and life story intersect with history; they assert that there is some kind of causal connection at work between our sense of individual identity and our social and cultural circumstances. In approaching generalizations such as these concerning the interface between the individual and society, we need to ask, how do such causal connections work, and what should we make of them? Focusing on autobiographical telling—specifically, on testimony in a judicial setting—William Chaloupka, as I suggested in chapter 1, invokes Michel Foucault's dark vision of individualism as a disciplinary practice of the state. Chaloupka's "Hood River John Doe" was the car thief who refused to tell the police who he was. Chaloupka comments, "Hood River John Doe's expressive silence—his temporary escape from identity—briefly illuminates how power now works, how successfully it captures and rearranges the seemingly simple, unproblematic fact of having an identity and expressing it" (389). I wonder, though: Is Chaloupka's resistant John Doe so much of an exception? As for me, although I am chastened by Foucault's insight into the workings of power, I side with the less-deterministic views of Gullestad and Hacking, for example, who read the exchange between individuals and the social structures they inhabit as a dialogic, give-and-take process. "People live their lives and tell their stories," Gullestad writes, "within socially structured conditions, but their actions and stories also have a potentially transformative impact on 'society'" (32).[3]

Well, I certainly like to think so, but I admit that it is challenging to conceptualize the relation between ourselves and our social environments, between our power to shape our selves and lives on the one hand, and on the other the forces that channel and check our freedom of action. Culture dwells in us for sure, but how does it dwell? Recalling the seventeenth-century letter writers painted by Ter Borch and Vermeer, I am remembering that Peter Sutton's introductory essay for the Bruce show catalog, with its comments on popular Dutch letter manuals, made me see the paintings in a new way. According to Sutton, when these apparently thoughtful letter writers sought to express themselves, they drew in part on prefabricated models of appropriate sentiments. The letter handbooks anticipate, as it were, the success of Hallmark cards today in supplying the content

3. Whereas Gullestad and Hacking conceive of the relation between the individual and the state as a dialogic, two-way process, Foucault gives a decidedly one-way account of this relation. In *Discipline and Punish* he argues that the emergence of new techniques of observation and description in hospitals and clinics at the end of the eighteenth century ushered in the possibility of subjecting the individual to the will of the state. In this view, individualism and the life writing associated with it show as instruments of state power: "For a long time ordinary individuality—the everyday individuality of everybody—remained below the threshold of description. To be looked at, observed, described in detail, followed from day to day by an uninterrupted writing was a privilege. The chronicle of a man, the account of his life, his historiography, written as he lived out his life formed part of the rituals of his power. The disciplinary methods reversed this relation, lowered the threshold of describable individuality and made of this description a means of control and a method of domination" (191).

and the form of feelings—Hallmark's motto, "Emotions are our business," is telling.[4] To recognize that the content of our so-called inner lives comes heavily freighted with material from outer sources is to send us back once more to the troubling connection between thoughts and things, between privacy and property. How much say do we have in fashioning what we have to say?

For quite a while now, in the wake of my reading in brain studies, I have believed that the physiological and neurological properties of our bodies could provide a kind of saving third term in the endless debates weighing free will against determinism. When our bodies are left out of account in such discussions, we can be made out to seem quite vulnerable, so much soft wax waiting to be stamped by the die press of culture. Isn't it a belief of this sort, for example, that plays into the chilling idea of brainwashing? Is the body, then, so porous and permeable, wide open to the pressures and influences of its environment? Against such a view, consider this bold assertion from the neurologist Gerald M. Edelman: "Your brain *constructs*. . . . It doesn't mirror. . . . Even before language, your brain constructs and makes perceptual slices of the world" (Levy 62). If Edelman is correct, we can say that in a certain profound neurological fashion, we make our realities. Yet part of that making may indeed involve mirroring. Study of "mirror neurons" in monkeys further complicates any understanding of the interface between self

4. See Sutton, esp. 34–37.

and culture: "When a monkey watches a researcher bring an object—an ice cream cone, for example—to his mouth, the same brain neurons fire as when the monkey brings a peanut to its own mouth." Commenting on the implications of this finding, the developmental psychologist Patricia Greenfield observes that whereas scholars have treated culture as fundamentally separate from biology, "now we see that mirror neurons absorb culture directly, with each generation teaching the next by social sharing, imitation and observation" (Blakeslee). Clearly we haven't heard the last word on the development of human culture, but making selves is part of this social and somatic process. Belief in individualism, which seems to authorize our confidence in our freedom to think, to act, to be what we want, to say who we are, needs to be measured against the constraints of culture that condition or otherwise set our possibilities.

Everyday Lives

I have tried to situate identity formation and the everyday narrative practices associated with it in the context of the cultures in which they unfold. More specifically, I believe that what I described in chapter 1 as a narrative identity system functions as it does at least in part because of its place in a larger economic structure. Think back to the example of Henry Mayhew's little watercress seller, and let her stand for the individual responding to the forces she perceives as shaping her life. This is my subject in the rest of this chapter, how people make sense of their experience, drawing on the models of self and life story available to them in their cultures. In the case of the watercress seller, it is likely that we have the eight-year-old child's story largely as she told it; we read her story, however, under the heading "Watercress Girl," slotted into the double columns of volume 1 of Mayhew's magisterial four-volume survey of the working class, *London Labour and the London Poor;* the watercress-girl narrative in its turn is placed under the rubric "Street-Sellers of Green Stuff," one of the major categories of "Sellers" who make up Mayhew's "Street-Folk." The child's story functions as a building block in Mayhew's ambitious program of classification, namely, "A Cyclopedia of the Condition and Earnings of Those That Will Work, Those That Cannot Work, And Those That Will Not Work." How should we read the isolated individual and her story, then, contained in the larger structure of an economic system? In constructing his typology of the world of work, Mayhew certainly seems to be engaged in that "making up" of persons that Ian Hacking describes as a characteristic bureaucratic activity of postindustrial states. In the diminishing perspective of this kind of social analysis, does the individual risk becoming a cipher, the self a statistic? Hacking's notion of a feedback loop assigns a label to a large-scale cultural process without really demonstrating how it functions. Can life writing in its various forms shed light on how this making up of persons works? Marianne Gullestad points the way in her study *Everyday Life Philosophers: Modernity, Morality, and Autobiography in Norway* (1996).

Taking my cue from Gullestad's title, I want to comment briefly first on the concept of "everyday life," for our customary associations of the commonplace, ordinary, and routine with the "everyday" carry with them the sense of "not worthy of note," with the result that we usually don't pay much attention to this nonetheless huge area of our experience.[5] Of all those who have tackled the everyday, I think that the French cultural anthropologist Michel de Certeau has been especially successful in bringing it into focus as an area of inquiry. Characterizing the members of a given culture as consumers, Certeau asks, "What do they make of what they 'absorb,' receive, and pay for? What do they do with it?" (31). This is the question Certeau sets out to answer in *The Practice of Everyday Life*. In his study of Certeau's work, Michael Sheringham stresses Certeau's conception of consumption as production. Countering the "alleged passivity" of individuals living in so-called consumer societies "in the face of the technocratic, bureaucratic and other systems that produce the goods, services, and environments in which consumption takes place," Sheringham underlines Certeau's belief that "consumption or use is in fact active and productive" (213). The everyday practices that Certeau targets include walking, reading, and speaking, and in every case, as Sheringham puts it, Certeau concludes that

5. Foucault dates the emergence of the everyday and the individual as objects of knowledge to the end of the eighteenth century (see note 3 above). Weintraub and other historians of autobiography date the rise of modern Western autobiography to this same period.

"users introduce creative play into the rigidities of ordering systems" (227).[6]

Marianne Gullestad contends, and I agree with her, that the activity of making selves and life stories is yet another everyday practice, and, like Certeau before her, she seeks "to understand the interplay between sociocultural structure and individual creativity" (31). Acknowledging the gap in much social science "between 'theory' provided by the scholar and 'data' provided by common people," she argues instead "that social life is theorized by those who live it" (307–8). To return to Hacking and his feedback-loop notion of what's involved in the process of "making up people," individuals in their ordinary lives emerge in this view as equal to those who study them. It is in this spirit that, in addition to considering three of the individuals whose stories Gullestad presents, I will also include a short version of my own life story, because I too am a player, like everyone else, in the narrative identity system that has been my subject in this book.

Gullestad seeks "to grasp and understand certain aspects of the structures within which people live their lives and from which they draw in making sense of their lives" (31). As she investigates how moral values are transmitted in twentieth-century Norwegian society, she opens up a fresh perspective on the social construction of selfhood. Refusing

6. I regard Sheringham's survey of the concept of everyday life in twentieth-century French thought as the best introduction I know of to this complex subject.

a deterministic view of the individual as passively shaped by social institutions, Gullestad sees individuals instead as engaged in a dynamic process of self-invention in which "they creatively refashion and adapt the knowledge, values, and ideas they receive" (31). For me, the key insight that emerges from Gullestad's research is that values contain the materials for building identity and life story.

Gullestad bases her findings on four autobiographies drawn from an archive of some 630 narratives, which she and the sociologist Reidar Almås gathered through a nationwide autobiography competition, "Write Your Life," held in Norway in 1988–1989.[7] While the use of an autobiography contest as an instrument of social and cultural analysis is not new—Gullestad points to similar projects in Poland and Finland (5)—what is new is Gullestad's interest in the textuality of the life stories that she and Almås collected in the "Write Your Life" project.[8] In *Everyday Life Philosophers* she approaches the contest narratives *as narratives* and not merely as quarries from which to extract quantifiable cultural information. As the historiographer Hayden White has argued, form itself is a content, and ought, accordingly, to be the object of historical inquiry. Gullestad and White are making a case for treating texts themselves

---

7. In their account of the contest and the methodology that informed it, Gullestad and Almås report that "the first prize was a journey for two to Greece," and that "all participants received a diploma." See "Write Your Life" 3.

8. The whole subject of autobiography contests is fascinating, and in addition to the commentaries Gullestad cites by Bertaux and Kohli, and Roos on this phenomenon, see also Lejeune, "Les instituteurs" (70–73), for a nineteenth-century French example, and "Archives" for a twentieth-century Italian one.

as facts endowed with social and historical significance. Although some social scientists may indeed refuse to accept the factuality of artifacts of this kind, cultural anthropologists such as Gullestad have made them the primary target of their research. Clifford Geertz, for example, identifies the ethnographer's concern as a study of "the symbolic forms...in terms of which, in each place, people actually represented themselves to themselves and to one another" ("From the Native's Point of View" 225).[9] Viewed in this perspective, autobiographies in particular and self-narration in general can give us Geertzian evidence of what individuals in a particular culture "perceive 'with'—or 'by means of,' or 'through'" ("From" 225). The contest autobiographies show individuals using cultural models of identity and life story—subsets of Geertz's "symbolic forms"—to make sense of their experience.

Where exactly do such models come from, and what is the manner of their dissemination? How do they achieve authority, and what are the institutions involved?[10] In the case of autobiography, for example, literary scholars have given literary answers to these questions, arguing that any book is

9. In a parallel fashion, Gullestad writes: "I am interested in the implicit cultural knowledge embodied in social practices. Culture is not a thing that human beings have, but an analytic aspect of their practices. I am, in other words, not only interested in what people think and do, but also in what they think and act with, i.e., the ideas, values, concepts, and beliefs that they routinely use as tools for thinking and acting" ("Reflections" 21).

10. See, e.g., Geertz, *Interpretation of Cultures,* and Bruner for research that proposes to answer these questions.

necessarily the product of the books that go before it.[11] Such theories of literary influence, however, omit any account of the transmission of texts as a primary cultural process. How, we should ask, do texts come to be as they are? For an answer, social scientists, especially cultural anthropologists and developmental psychologists, direct our attention to the ways in which institutions—notably family, school, and church—contribute to the formation of the individual's subjectivity. Complementing this familiar picture of the cultural sources of identity and life story—literary texts, social institutions—is Gullestad's stress on values. "Constructions of self and identity," she observes, "are...dependent upon moral notions" (20). Taking Gullestad's key insight that values are repositories of form, I want to extend her analyses by exploring the narrative structures that emerge in the value dilemmas faced by three of her "everyday philosophers"—Einar, Kari, and Øivind.[12] Latent in the discourses used to express a culture's values, I argue, are metaphors for self and life story, rudiments of plot and character that individuals draw on as they live their lives and—sometimes—write them. These three simple narratives help us to understand how the phenomenon that Ian Hacking calls "making up people" works.

11. See, e.g., Fleishman, who traces the history of autobiographical "figures," the "verbal formulas, iconographic images and intellectual commonplaces" that cumulatively, over the centuries, constitute what he calls "the lingua franca of literary discourse" (49).

12. I should caution that my knowledge of the "Write Your Life" contest materials that I discuss here is derived exclusively from Gullestad's presentation of them. I am, as it were, reading over her shoulder, at one remove from the primary sources.

Einar titles his autobiography "My Childhood and Youth in a Periphery of the Periphery," whereas Gullestad titles her analysis of it "Einar: From Fisherman to Bureaucrat." The disjunction between the two titles—the opposing narrative destinations—is immediately apparent and instructive. On the face of it, Einar's move from a "peripheral," marginalized Sami fishing community to a clerical job, marriage, and family life in the city has all the markings of the conventional success story, and Gullestad likens it to the trajectory of the traditional bildungsroman (115), a novel that follows an individual's growth from childhood to maturity, exploring the tension between the desire for self-development and the constraints of social roles. Einar, however, in a statement of life purpose remarkable for its negatives, insists that he rejected a developmental story of this kind: "I left fishing in order to get something to do, not in order to make a career. I never made a career and, this is also not what I set out to do" (120).[13] Nor does he write that story of career: "After you marry and have a family of your own, you go to and fro and there is nothing much to write about" (117).

In place of the unwritten bildungsroman, Einar writes what Gullestad characterizes as a narrative of apology to justify why he had to abandon the traditional Sami way of life he had known as a child (106). Reconstructing his situation

---

13. It may be merely an effect of translation, but the statement "I never made a career, and this is also not what I set out to do" (120) has an interesting and perhaps revealing ambiguity about it: (1) I never made a career, and I never intended to; (2) I never made a career *but* this is not what I intended. In any case, the conflicted discourse strikes me as characteristic of Einar and his marginal identity situation.

at the decisive moment of vocation, Einar presents himself as a marginal, transitional individual caught between two models of identity, two ways of life, affiliating with neither, yet accepting to his own discomfort the terms of the conventional model of career and success which he nonetheless did not choose to embrace.[14] He writes of his peers that "they went to school in order to 'become somebody,'" while he "was still at home and remained 'nobody'" (104). The long and short of it, however, is that Einar *did do something,* but it wasn't "a career" and it wasn't fishing, which he wasn't interested in and which made him sick. As I see it, Einar's story is finally neither a bildungsroman nor an apology, although it contains elements of both; it is really something else, something moreover that perhaps the autobiography contest itself assisted him to work through and construct, what I would term a *narrative of disaffiliation.* I see him as between stories—Gullestad suggests this to me when she speaks of him as "commuting" (121) between two ways of life.[15] Einar does not enter *narratively* into either one. Thus he may have enacted a developmental trajectory in his living, but it is largely unrepresented in his telling, while he focuses his counternarrative of his childhood world precisely

14. This acceptance of the terms of the model he does not embrace is echoed in the title he chooses for his story as well: "My Childhood and Youth in a Periphery of the Periphery."

15. Gullestad interprets Einar's situation rather differently, contending that he maintains a double affiliation with both the old life he left behind and the new life he made for himself in the city. He develops, she suggests, a "commuting, hybrid self" (personal communication to the author). For further insight into this notion of cultural "commuting," see Gullestad, "Reflections."

on the moment when he decides to abandon it. I want to look briefly at this unusually rich passage, which Gullestad identifies as a pivotal "'moment of interpretation'" (110) leading to a decisive, existentialist choice of life project.

As he stands looking out to sea, reflecting on his life, Einar seems to identify with the freedom of birds making their way in a hostile environment: "the fulmar bird flying in the storm" and "the black-backed gull which...had started to search for a travel space and probably told me with some juicy expressions in black-backed gull language that he was first" (110). The black-backed gull models for Einar a solitary alter ego who possesses a positive identity ("first") and the will to enact its capacities ("search for a travel space"), an identity endowed with the possibility of action and the language with which to express it in a story. What I am suggesting is that Einar may have found a therapeutic opening in the "Write Your Life" contest, a "travel space" in which to express self and life-course not in the conventional language of the bildungsroman or the apology but in a "black-backed gull language" of resistance: he makes a model of the lack of model from which he suffered as a young man, telling his story and in so doing making himself not "somebody" in the "career" sense but *someone with a story to tell.* Gullestad's analysis and publication of this non-story story, moreover, validates it as a life narrative, giving it status and standing. I suspect, in fact, that the contest and subsequent scholarly commentary have answered to the contestants' need for validation and recognition. In the context of contemporary Norway's "transformed modernity" (10–14), its increasingly secularized culture, doubtless it was deeply satisfying for the contestants to know that someone was paying attention to them, not only reading them but talking and writing about them: they were worthy subjects of research for credentialed academic professionals such as Almås and Gullestad.

The mismatch between the cultural resources for identity formation and the individual's circumstances, which I believe Einar experienced as a kind of double displacement, an existence on the "periphery of the periphery" as he calls it, is experienced by Kari, in the second of Gullestad's "everyday life" autobiographies, as a psychological breakdown requiring hospitalization. Her therapist apparently concluded that Kari was too dependent, that she had failed to achieve a suitably adult measure of autonomy. Kari herself believes that she had become ill "because she had several 'not so good characteristics'" (173)—in Kari's own understanding of her situation, character and value have become inextricably intertwined. Indeed, the value structure of Kari's story is simple and striking: a focal episode in youth in which she accepts a guiding life principle, followed in midlife by a psychological crisis in which this principle is disconfirmed.

Kari herself makes the connection between the two episodes. Although she finds herself at thirteen suddenly adrift and on her own when her grandmother dies, she is sustained by a piece of the grandmother's advice that "came to determine most of the years of my life": "'If I should pass away, and you are in doubt about what to do, then try to think of what I would have told you.'" The role of the other in this self-defining moment is central, yet the grandmother's advice, despite its apparent call for deference, functions simultaneously as a rationale for independence and autonomy. Kari makes this point clearly when, recalling the day of her grandmother's burial, she observes, "I felt a kind of self-confidence." In what would become a pattern for Kari, this recognition of autonomy dawns as a kind of authoritative instruction from the other, "now childhood is over and you have to start taking care of yourself" (134). Although Kari's therapist failed to grasp it, the grandmother herself was apparently a quite complex figure who, despite her associations with hearth and home, encouraged Kari to "'reach out for something better'" (152)—better, for example, than working in a factory. Kari clearly understood her grandmother's empowering call to be more ambitious: "I fought my way upwards and forwards, the way Grandmother recommended" (156).

The pattern of independent action in the guise of obedience to advice is repeated when Kari recalls her decision to adopt a more refined style of speech despite family criticism. Relationally conditioned, she fights family with family in a decisive moment of introspection before her mirror, in which, again, we hear Kari in "thought-correspondence with Grandmother" (174): "'You are going to manage on your own, Kari, and you are going to behave in such a way that nobody will have any reason to blame you'" (153). Kari will achieve autonomy in obedience to the other, and it is precisely the anticipated approval of the other that authorizes her budding individualism. Kari instinctively embraces the paradox of her grandmother's life-defining advice: she had been given permission to be herself.

Which brings me to the therapist who treated her during her midlife breakdown—a flat-footed figure who comes off rather badly in Kari's account. This patronizing fellow, the voice of the institution at its prescriptive worst, tells her that she "had never made an independent decision all [her] life," and Kari, ever obedient to the voice of authority, seems to accept the therapist's view that her grandmother "had decided [her] life," although she immediately qualifies this admission by saying, "It was probably not her intention." The therapist proceeds to enact the authoritarian posture he had criticized in the grandmother as damaging to Kari's self-esteem: "'Now let us put Grandmother away here, and let her rest in peace.'" Notwithstanding the smug condescension of the therapist's "now let us," Kari reports that his request "sounded like an order, and believe it or not, she [the grandmother] disappeared from me" (174).

Gullestad's delicate and discriminating analysis of the role of the grandmother in Kari's life and decision making underlines the simplistic nature of the therapist's interpretation: what he had seen as dependence was rather a way of "grounding moral decisions in popular forms of knowledge transmitted orally in important social relations" (174). There is an important difference, she argues, between obedience and responsibility, defining the responsible individual as "somebody who acts in terms of deeply held and actively chosen moral values and convictions" (176). In this case, Grandmother really did know best, best for Kari at any rate, and Kari eventually confided to Gullestad that she had resumed her "thought-correspondence" with her grandmother: "I have brought her forth again, and that's fine" (175). Perhaps, in the relational world of Kari's child-hood, the call to individualism could reach her only in the form of the advice the grandmother gave her, the grand-mother who bridged two worlds, who was both worker and homemaker, who "reached out for something better" for Kari.

Gullestad identifies two "ideal structures" (181) in Kari's autobiography, a chronological life-course plot from child-hood to advanced age and an "attempt to achieve complete-ness" through the performance of the autobiographical act itself. Gullestad's analysis makes me see a third structur-ing element in value itself and in its transmission, for the transmission of value is a major theme in so many of the episodes she analyzes. It is especially noteworthy that in the grandmother's admonition, Kari is enjoined to imagine "what I would have told you"; she was invited to imag-ine the grandmother giving her advice without the advice being specified. And Kari is herself notably preoccupied with the transmission of value, not merely in "thought-correspondence" with her grandmother but also, in her turn, in her views on child rearing and on the writing of her autobiography, for she desires to transmit her story to her descendants. What is important to Kari is to locate a value-appropriate language, a course of conduct that will be "blameless." Her search for a language of self-expression, as Gullestad makes clear, is made more difficult by the therapist's delegitimation of the grandmother's in-fluence and values during the most impressionable period of Kari's youth.

Nevertheless, while the therapist's diagnosis seems simplistic, it is also true that Kari *was* sick, and Gullestad hypothesizes that her ailments—and perhaps those especially of women—represent a "somatisation" of social and cultural experience that affords Kari a "vocabulary" to articulate her suffering (149). Kari's illness functions for her as the "black-backed gull language" had for Einar, expressing experience that the familiar discourses of the culture and its institutions contrive to silence. Despite the reductive nature of Kari's view that her breakdown was caused by "several 'not so good characteristics,'" it points nonetheless to a fundamental perception that emerges from this autobiography: that value may supply both a model of identity and a plot for life-story action.

The "Write Your Life" autobiographies testify to the creativity of the ordinary person. As might be expected, these narratives display the imprint of the culture and its institutions on the individual's sense of identity. At the same time, however, each narrative reworks shared cultural material in unique and distinctive ways. Einar locates a life story between stories in a narrative of disaffiliation, while Kari struggles to claim her story as her own in the face of the therapist's charge that her grandmother "had decided [her] life." By contrast, Øivind, the third and in many ways the most interesting of Gullestad's "everyday life philosophers," emerges as a man who never mustered the courage to embrace the story that would have realized his youthful ambitions: in the memorable final image of his narrative, Øivind exposes the "black holes" lurking beneath his treasured childhood "memories" (219); autobiography and the identity it confers open onto a void.

Gullestad discerns in Øivind's narrative a "three-layered model of society," a model, she contends, that many Norwegians subscribe to today: in the middle are "people like us," who "stick together," determined not to "sink down" to the level of the poor, while the few, the rich, "stand out" on top. In addition, and complementing this three-layered vertical model, she detects a binary set of value oppositions between inside and outside, between home and the world beyond, and so forth (198–99). Implicit in the metaphoric structure of this value system is a series of life-course plots, those risings and fallings of economic and social status that are the stuff of Ibsen's plays. How, exactly, are such models communicated to a child? To the young Øivind, for example?

Øivind is thirteen when he takes a full-time job in order to assist his mother in supporting their family in straitened circumstances—"we were three to provide for six"; this step foreclosed his chance for an education and his vague dreams of the future. When the aging autobiographer reconstructs this turning point in the life of his younger self, he draws precisely on the metaphoric potential for action latent in the three-tier model of society: "The bold ones can break out, rise towards the surface and become their own decision makers. But not me. The family in No. 25 became my destiny. I was part of it" (206). Self and life story, act and character, become interchangeable in this moment of choice that isn't choice, which follows the logic of the boy's passive model of selfhood: he is someone to whom things happen, someone who does not really choose (214). It is scarcely surprising, then, that Øivind's narrative terminates with the end of his childhood, and Gullestad notes that Øivind's story, unlike Kari's and Einar's, lacks a "specific interpretive moment in which the young man takes charge of his life and formulates an explicit life project of his own" (208).

There are, however, what I would term two "anti-interpretive" moments, episodes in which the youth does *not* take charge of his life but accepts instead the role he believes his family has assigned him, an acceptance that lays the groundwork for his embracing at age thirteen his sense of their project for him as his own. In these two passages we see the boy trust in what he has been given, in what has been "chosen" for him. Probing Øivind's story, Gullestad concludes that "*something* in him was preventing him from making the choice that would give him an education, and thereby a chance to 'rise to the surface'" (208, emphasis added). What was that "something"? The two "anti-interpretive," self-and-story-determining moments point to an answer.

The first of these moments concerns the child—now able to open the heavy gate—as he begins to cross the boundary between home and the world: "*Don't go too far. Be careful,*" he was warned, and Øivind himself treats this admonition metaphorically, interpreting it as foreshadowing the destiny of the older self who "took no risks." Gullestad emphasizes the moral values of restraint, control, and care in the mother's warning; not going "too far" becomes for her "a meta-level description" of Øivind's reticence about his most intimate concerns in the autobiography as a whole

(200–1). Gullestad's stress on the "symbolic tensions between inside and outside" (201) opens up additional registers of meaning: don't succeed, don't "stand out"; stick with us, and you will be rewarded with love and security (this last is Øivind's own point). That is to say that these daily admonitions functioned as a dress rehearsal for the turning point at age thirteen, a turning point in name only, for, figuratively and psychologically speaking, Øivind was the boy who didn't turn out into the world but remained at home, behind the gate.

"*Don't go too far*"—all this may seem like a heavy freight of interpretation for the simple language of the parent's warning to bear, but Gullestad's analyses here and throughout *Everyday Life Philosophers* make an excellent case for recognizing in the transmission of values the seeds of identity and story that structure our self-narratives. Øivind focuses our attention on his going in and out through the gate accompanied by his mother's voice, and he proceeds to set in motion the whole set of metaphoric interpretations I have just rehearsed. Going in and out through the gate may seem rather trivial, but I suspect that it is precisely through the medium of frequently performed, habitual actions that values are most likely to be transmitted. The very nature of the action, its daily repetition, its simplicity, suggest that the metaphoric charge it gradually acquired for Øivind developed in the most natural way. Observing Gullestad observe Øivind, I conclude, this is what the transmission of value looks like from the vantage point of experience.

If we seek to identify the sources of the principal large-scale metaphors of autobiography, of self and life story, we need to pay attention to the story-making potential of the values Gullestad examines in these narratives—"reaching out for something better," "sinking down," "standing out," "going far," and so forth. We need to read the figures backward to their grounding in experience. In *Metaphors We Live By,* George Lakoff and Mark Johnson argue that metaphors are not merely distinctive features of the language we use to express thought; instead, they argue, "human *thought processes*" themselves are "largely metaphorical" (6, emphasis in original). Believing that metaphors "structure how we perceive, how we think, and what we do" (4), they proceed to create a typology of the metaphors that organize our lives. In every case they locate the origins of metaphor in cultural and especially in physical, bodily experience, and metaphors of value, I would add, are no exception. If we live by metaphors, we also write our lives by them, and these autobiographies show us this process of self-construction at work.

Now I want to look at the second of the two "anti-interpretive moments": Øivind's painful recollection of a childhood disappointment. Gullestad interprets this particular Christmas memory as an authentic expression of the child's point of view. In general, she acknowledges that in an autobiography memories will necessarily be colored by the perspective of the remembering adult, but she singles out this one as allowing a glimpse of the boy Øivind had been both because of its unusual emotional intensity ("the story's strongest") and because it "does not quite fit into the general theme" of Øivind's narrative (213).[16] Øivind recalls sitting around the Christmas tree on Christmas Eve and his excitement before opening his present from his father, for he tells us that "we expected most from the presents from father." The present proves to be "a big, stylish, marzipan figure," and Øivind bites off the head, only to discover that it was made out of soap. The bitter disappointment and humiliation are simply and sharply declared as a series of blows: "Father laughed! Everybody laughed. At me!" (211–12). I agree with Gullestad that the experience touched a nerve in the child that continues to ache a lifetime later, but I would stress the dialogic interplay between the child Øivind and the aging autobiographer. As she points out, it is the adult with his literary strategies who invests this memory with special significance (the repetitions and so forth), and we should ask why. What is behind his pouring so much literary energy into representing the child's disappointment?

The rest of Øivind's narrative makes me suspect that *he* suspects that his thirteen-year-old self had been betrayed by his family when he made the life-defining decision to give up his education and start working to help support them: he had chosen a marzipan figure that proved to be made out of soap. It is as though the youth had been tricked by the adults, conned into accepting their values, which they didn't

16. Although Gullestad detects the adult's retrospective presence in the literary language and strategies used to reconstruct the episode, she believes nonetheless that "we are closer to Øivind the child in this passage than anywhere else in the story"; that the child's emotion "has not grown old but has kept its raw vitality and force" (213).

themselves believe in, just as, earlier, the child had been betrayed by the father. In this reading, then, the Christmas memory is also a replay—as is the entire narrative—of the choice that wasn't a choice, the choice to stick with and support the family.[17] If my hunch is correct, then Øivind's story is a peculiarly painful one, in which the autobiographer confronts his doubts about the moral grounding of the life he has lived and the self he has become. If I am right, then the entire narrative functions as the "interpretive moment" Gullestad finds missing in Øivind's tale. Gullestad believes that Øivind's primary motive for writing his narrative of childhood was that "out of his experiences during these years he was able to create a pattern describing his self that seemed to hold for the next six decades" (221). Perhaps, but the marzipan deception—at least *as Øivind now recalls it*— seems to disconfirm the pattern, and I think it is telling that the final sentences of the narrative should repeat in capsule form the expectation/disappointment, marzipan/soap tension that structures the Christmas memory: speaking of the house in which he had spent his childhood, he writes: "And it is filled with memories. And black holes" (219).[18]

---

17. Gullestad links this memory to another moment in which Øivind portrays himself as a child who suspects "that somebody *little* does not understand everything the big ones understand" (213). If she is correct in making this connection, the passage would seem to support the interpretive weight that Øivind, Gullestad, and I have given to the marzipan episode: the autobiographer portrays the child as intuiting the existence of a latent kernel of meaning that he lacks the power to articulate.

18. Gullestad argues that Øivind "oscillated" between two views of himself, such that the marzipan deception does not so much disconfirm his "pattern" or model of identity but is rather a part of it. I come back to what strikes me as a highly charged image: Øivind's linking of memory with "black holes." I note an

Cultural anthropologists attempt to identify the tools we use to organize and understand our experience. Prominent among these tools are certain primary sense-making categories, including concepts of time and of the person. Drawing on these categories, autobiographers (re)construct their lives, and the cultural anthropologist who proposes to use such material as a source for social analysis must ask—and here I return to the questions I posed earlier—where does the individual's sense of self and life story come from? Gullestad's studies of her "everyday life philosophers" reveal the models of identity that are coded in a culture's values, models that precipitate out in the autobiographies elicited by the "Write Your Life" contest. Working over her autobiographers' texts with patience and tact, she teases key value words back to their origins in everyday discourse, discourses spoken in schools and churches but especially in families. In particular, Gullestad makes me see the self-and-narrative potential of what we *say* we believe—"don't go too far," "stick together," "stand out," and so forth. Her study of the transmission of these values shows how social institutions are *experientially* linked to the individual: "Values," she urges, "do not only exist as explicit notions, but may also be reproduced in subtle

---

interesting gap between what Øivind wrote and the impression he seems to have made on Gullestad in his subsequent conversations with her about his life and narrative. The follow-up interviews with the informants obviously enrich and complement the written narratives in interesting ways, but I suspect that they also raise problems for ethnographic interpretation that are not easily solved. In this case, for example, I would suggest that Øivind may have been prepared to own in writing a starker interpretation of his life than he was prepared to own to Gullestad in person.

ways through embodied practices in everyday life" (265). Sensitizing us to recognize these "embodied practices" that make up the texture of the quotidian, Gullestad puts us in a good position to recognize how identity formation functions as a cultural process.

In making so much of Øivind's going back and forth through the gate, however, his movement toward autonomy disciplined by the cautionary parental injunction not to go "too far," I don't want to embrace some impossible quest for origins. We can never expect to witness the emergent sense of self, of life story, as an observable event, for it is an ongoing process. The datable moments—Einar standing by the sea, Kari standing in front of her mirror, Øivind biting into the marzipan figure—are explicit or implicit moments of recognition that the sense of self and its story has *already* taken a decisive turn; we never catch ourselves in the act of *becoming selves.* We are always out of sync with our selves, always lagging behind, always trying to catch up retrospectively. Thus, the autobiographies Gullestad studies are themselves attempts to recapture the decisive moments in which the autobiographers believe they became what they think they are. But self, of course, which we take to be experiential fact, is also finally a fiction, an elusive creature that we construct even as we seek to encounter it. Even when we train an ethnographic gaze on ourselves, even when we are our own subjects, our own informants, there is always a gap or rupture that divides us from the knowledge that we seek.

If I were to speculate about why Gullestad chose the autobiographies she did for analysis out of the hundreds in the contest archive, I would guess that she is especially drawn to individuals who find themselves at odds with their culture's received values. When I asked her about this pattern in her fieldwork, she commented, "I found that the best informants were often people who were a little marginal in the group: they were able to make explicit the general rules for inclusion and exclusion, for example, in ways that more centrally located individuals were not. I think that there is a general point here—that cultural values and ideas are best studied at the margins and in interstices between institutions and groups."[19] Not quite fitting in, as in the cases of Einar and Kari, or fitting in too well, as in the case of Øivind, generates an uncomfortable—and revealing— self-consciousness about models of self and life story that we are usually scarcely aware of because we take them for granted. Kari, for example, notes a shift in identity models from "being of use," a formulation characteristic of her own 1950s childhood that she linked to the idea of obedience, to "being oneself," a model she proposes for her daughter's formation forty years later (285–86). Kari's struggle with being herself confirms the importance of what Gullestad calls "categories of belonging," including "kinship, home, locality, nationality, and religion" (292), which help define "anchorage points for the self" (285). Being oneself might

---

19. Personal communication to the author. Making a case for the importance of neglected working-class lives and life stories in Britain, the historian Carolyn Steedman takes a similar position. "Lives lived out on the borderlands," she writes, make conveniently visible a culture's "central interpretative devices" precisely because they don't square with them (*Landscape for a Good Woman* 5).

seem to be self-evident, something on the order of a label rather than a project, but as Kari's story suggests, individuals may be obliged to find this self in order to be it. Her internalization of cultural values reflected in her imagined dialogues with her grandmother, and her desire to align her own experience with her sense of approved models, lead to her unsettling recognition that she was not cut out to play the part she thought had been assigned to her: she had "several 'not so good characteristics.'" The primary activity that connects Kari, Einar, and Øivind—different as they are—is precisely this kind of measuring: they measure themselves and their lives against what they think their culture expects of them.

"What they think their culture expects them of them"—I have been suggesting that the measuring of self and life-course in these stories involves social and cultural expectations. In *The Self in Moral Space,* drawing on the work of the philosopher Charles Taylor, David Parker persuades me that this measuring that motivates life writing is necessarily a work of moral evaluation as well: "Life narrators," he urges, "feel a need to speak from a moral orientation they take to be right" (87), centering on the question *"what is it good to be?"* (98, emphasis in original). The stories of Einar, Kari, and Øivind certainly seem to support Parker's claim. What I find especially moving is that these ordinary, otherwise unknown individuals should have responded to the "Write Your Life" contest as an opportunity not only to take stock of what they had done with their lives but to exhibit their findings to a public gaze without flinching.

"I...remained 'nobody,'" Einar writes, "you go to and fro and there is nothing much to write about." And Øivind, the boy who didn't "go far," and Kari, who never thought she "was something"—it is remarkable how unsparing they are in their judgments of themselves. There is something of an ache in these everyday lives, a sense of missed opportunities, a current of lack. Yet Parker contends that the upshot of this life measuring is ultimately positive: "If, as [Charles] Taylor argues, it is a condition of being a functioning self that I speak from a moral orientation I take to be right, I simply *cannot* narrate the story by which I came to ultimate epistemic loss" (78, emphasis in original). To clarify Parker's point, I should add that he defines Taylor's notion of "epistemic gain" as "a new way of seeing things that constitutes a gain over the previous one" (77). So what is the gain for Einar, Kari, and Øivind?

While the content of these stories may have left me with a sense of lack, it is important to take into account as well the telling of these stories and the self-understanding and self-acceptance that go with it. As I said in chapter 1, successful performance of self-narration, considered socially, establishes us as normal individuals; additionally—and this is my point here—it can confirm that we have led interesting lives and are, accordingly, interesting people who are worthy of respect from others. I think we do pay attention to the notion that our lives are interesting and hence valuable, something we measure by monitoring the reception we get when we talk about them with others. I think we crave the kind of validation that reception of our stories, told and written, can provide. Moreover, I believe that lurking somewhere in the telling of any life story is a facing down of mortality, the will to say that one's life has left a trace, that any self and life have value.

I think that this validation that the act of telling or writing lives confers sheds light on the otherwise puzzling phenomenon of the failed life. Consider the case of the "disappointed" individual. This is a label that I hear applied now and then to someone in mid- to late life whose "promise" seems somehow to have been unfulfilled. It is definitely a question of measuring: "promise" operates as shorthand for a plot or life-course of value, and when we say that someone is "disappointed," we are not merely saying that we think this person has failed but that we suspect this person thinks so too—this is what hurts, the thought that we or anyone could have reached a point in our lives where there are no second chances left. Had Øivind settled for a mess of pottage? Was the therapist right when he told Kari that her grandmother had "decided" her life for her? To judge one's life so harshly—and both Øivind and Kari explicitly entertain that possibility—is potentially much more devastating than admissions of failure by those who are otherwise famous and obviously successful—I am thinking of F. Scott Fitzgerald's confession of his "crack-up" in the pages of *Esquire,* for example; of Jean-Paul Sartre's claim in *The Words* that his adult life and career were based on a mistake; of Henry Adams's notorious—and learned—assertion in *The Education of Henry Adams* that he had never learned or accomplished anything of value. In all these cases, great and small, it is the self-understanding implied by the very act of making the life in narrative that redeems or protects it from any possible construction as a failure.

Thinking about Gullestad's "everyday life philosophers" and about Parker's study of the ethics of life writing, I began to see myself and my own life story as implicated in the case I have been making: we are all players in a narrative identity system. Like everyone else, I had to have a story, and my problem seemed to be, like Einar's, that mine turned out to be what I thought of as a non-story story. While I saw myself as ordinary and conventional, I felt at odds with my circumstances nonetheless because I couldn't fit in comfortably. I kept waiting for my life, which I regarded as a story of vocation, to play out as such stories commonly do, and when it didn't, the psychological friction produced the personal narrative that follows.

" 'My Father...' "

A few years ago I happened to read a little gem of a book, *Messages from My Father,* by Calvin Trillin. It is a simple, plainspoken story, and in the later chapters, where he writes about his father's failing health, quite moving. The evocation of growing up in the 1950s really hit home. Trillin is only three years older than I am, and his high school yearbook picture on the dust jacket looks like mine: close-cropped hair, face airbrushed and unsmiling, stiff pose in sport coat and tie. I was struck by his account of all that he and his father didn't say to each other. Here is Trillin on riding in the car with his dad: "In fact, the drives often passed in complete silence. I don't think either of us considered that odd. We took it for granted that men were, by nature, stoic." Reticence runs deep, I thought, in the Midwest. So many things come together in Trillin's story: the immigrant experience, his Jewish heritage, his choice of vocation, the setting (Kansas City). Ultimately, too, the book is a portrait of the artist as a young man, and we can see the connections between the father's plain style—blunt, stubborn—and the son's—more elegant; after all, he went to Yale, as his father had hoped. Trillin presents his father as a model of a certain kind of man, whose idea for his own life and for his son's is focused intensely on the American dream of success: "My father's Grand Plan, I think, began with my going to Yale—not on a shoestring, but in the way the sons of the industrialists went to Yale. I would then be not simply a real American, unencumbered by poverty and Old World views, but a privileged American—an American whose degree could give him a place on some special, reservations-only escalator to success." Despite his differences, the son embraces that model. "After that," Trillin writes, "it was up to me."

I kept thinking about Trillin's memoirs—*Messages from My Father* and *Remembering Denny*—in the days that followed this reading. How interesting they were, connecting deeply with my own life: the midwesterner going east in the '50s—the burden of expectations—the success plot. The books drive home the contrast between Calvin—or "Bud" as he was called—and his classmate and close friend

Denny: family and especially father standing behind Bud, and the absence of father (or any family) in Denny's sad case. Denny's story reads almost like Dick Diver's in F. Scott Fitzgerald's great novel, *Tender Is the Night:* peaking early as an icon of Ivy League success in a spread in *Life* magazine about his graduation from Yale, Denny ended, midcareer, in suicide. All this set me to thinking about my own father. There were a lot of things I had never really worked out about Dad's dreams of success, for himself and for me. I wondered why the right moment to do so had been so long in coming; I had a sense of switches turning on day and night.

In particular, I started brooding about an event that had occurred three years before at a family wedding. As parents of the groom, my wife and I arrived early for the final event, a reception hosted by the bride's parents. As we entered the reception, the bride's father took me aside and told me that it was a Jewish custom to remember the absent dead on such occasions. He asked me to say something about my father, who had died twenty years earlier, and I agreed. At the appointed moment, I rose to speak to the assembled guests. "My father...," I began, and then I could say no more. Somehow unprovided, I stood there gazing at all those upturned faces waiting to hear what I had to say. It was as though two hands were squeezing my heart, leaving me winded and speechless. Eventually I collected myself. I have no memory of what I said. What I do remember is my not being able to speak, to fill the huge gulf of silence. The surge of raw emotion caught me completely by surprise. Dad had been dead for more than twenty years. Surely his story was over, and his story for me as well. What kept me from speaking? What was it that I couldn't say?

Only six months before this event I thought I had said everything there was to say about me and Dad. One of my life writing students, a brilliant young man who edited an undergraduate literary magazine, had been after me to write the story of my life. "I'll give you a thousand words," he said. Some story! I boasted afterward that I had pulled it off in a single page. Here is what I wrote:

Not a Story

Why not write your story? he asks. You tell him, evasively, you've already written it obliquely by writing about others' lives. But he persists: you told us that everyone has a story. You believe this, you tell him. One makes choices; one shapes one's life. Also, you don't believe this. Isn't it culture calling the shots, displaying its wares, its models of identity, of life story? This is what you can do and be, this and this and this; not that. Time's story-arrow is flying all the while.

My father, self-made man in the American grain, thought he had missed the education he wanted, the one his admired business partner had had. This cultivated gentleman, member of an elegant local literary society, had gone to Exeter and Harvard. My father's dream: if my brothers and I would go to these schools, he would pay for it. We went.

Once I had completed his story, I needed to start my own. (It had started a long time before, on day one; I didn't know that; I thought my life would start after I got out of school.)

So what are you going to do with the rest of your life? they asked. By senior year everyone seemed to know the answer to that one; everyone had reached a turning in the road, the calling to some lifework. One friend claimed he had known what he wanted to do and be since he was eight. Eight! And I at eight who did not know; nor at eighteen; nor at twenty-two. I didn't think my life was a story like that; it wasn't really convincing.

I went to Paris for cover—"studying abroad," I thought, would do. My French friends, though, were puzzled by my unstoried, careerless state; nor could they afford it. There were dusty lectures at the venerable Sorbonne; there were also cafés along the Boulevard Saint Germain and the Rue des Ecoles. Du Bellay, Mallarmé, and wonderful coffee—my hands would shake after so many cups. I begin to drift. (It's true what they say about cafés.) I move from the Cité Universitaire to a small hotel in the Latin Quarter; I drink calvados on cold days. A professor, whose class I have been cutting, confronts me the day I return, bronzed, from skiing in the Alps: *"Ah, M. Eakin, vous êtes là ce matin! Vous étiez souffrant?" "Non, pas tellement,"* I reply. And then Italy in April, and Greece in May and June—there were so many antiquities, so many days. I was forgetting my French degree.

Embarrassed by the pointlessness of my existence, I headed back to school, back to Harvard; I was going backwards. I didn't really believe in it and suspected I would be found out. Graduate study in English was a new angle—I had never taken any courses in English literature before. The other students, earnest, dutiful and advanced, were checking out the Silver Poets (I never got to them), while I, mere novice, settled for the greats, for Chaucer, Spenser, Shakespeare, Milton, and so on down the line. I wasn't confident I would pass the doctoral entrance exam at the end of the year; I didn't paint my apartment on the unfashionable back side of Beacon Hill. Why bother, when I would be out of this story come June and into the army and off to Vietnam? Midyear I went into a stall; I couldn't write another paper; my father was slipping into a long and irreversible illness; I knew my teacher-story was not the one he had hoped for; I wept; I wrote another paper, and another; I was going to write papers for the rest of my life.

I passed the exam, and on I went. I was still waiting, though, for that elusive story-confirming experience of vocation to make it right. It never came. Instead, I kept wading on and on; I was in deep now; I started to swim; I am still swimming. Too late for stories now.

When I wrote that version of my relation to Dad, I was concerned with vocation, with his having chosen a story for me—something on the order of Abe Trillin's having fixed on a *Stover at Yale* success plot for son Calvin—and with my failure to complete that story in the way he would have wished. I am convinced that the issue of vocation was central between us, even though we never talked about it—I had the sense that college teaching was not quite "it" for him, second best, not truly one of the Professions. If I didn't have the story appointed for me by my father, did that mean I didn't have a story? *Not a Story:* I see now that Dad was calling the shots more than twenty years after his death. Fathers choose our stories for us, I must have believed this, and if we refuse the choice we go without.

But there was a lot I didn't say in *Not a Story.* To begin with, there was my shock when I saw Dad in Paris at the end of that year of escape. He'd recently been diagnosed with Parkinson's disease after months of baffling symptoms, and despite his impeccable dress—his polished shoes, his tie and handkerchief just so, not a hair out of place—the progress of the malady was unmistakable. I remember how he hated Versailles, where the graveled paths made the sound of his dragging feet so obvious.

And then there's what I called my "stall." *I wept*—those two words that functioned for me as the climax of my guarded, minimalist autobiography—that's supposed to tell it all. I didn't, for example, talk about my visit to a psychiatrist at the end of my first semester of graduate school. I remember how hard it was to get up my courage to make the appointment, and how annoyed I was that I couldn't be seen immediately. When I went, it all poured out, words and tears. It was all about Dad. I was amazed afterward at how quickly everything seemed to clear up. Later, when I ran into the psychiatrist in the street, I felt a deep dislike for him, and turned away.

The obvious point of *Not a Story* is my difficulty in coming to terms with my difference from my father; that's what plays into my "stall," my sense of wanting my father's blessing, my suspicion that he didn't believe in what I was proposing to do with my life. Yet in surprising ways I think I am like Dad. It is not just our shared looks, or even our handwriting (my signature is coming to look more and more like his). Our initials are the same, too, but our middle names are different—he was Paul James and I am Paul John—so I am not "Junior," a source of lifelong confusion; we are and are not alike. My parents never meant to call me Paul, and so my full name, above all my first name, the name I kept out of respect for Dad when I began to publish, has always seemed like a kind of disguise. I wonder whether this is connected—vocation again—to my deep-seated sense of imposture, that I wasn't really good enough—"good enough" to be "Paul"?—that sooner or later I would be found out. When I read reviews of my work, even now, I sometimes have the odd sense that they might be about someone else, and when they are good, that I would like to meet this guy.

But Dad didn't live to know anything of my work on autobiography and life writing, which became my lifework only after he was dead. What he knew dates from an earlier time, when he was relentlessly slipping into the grip of Parkinson's. The malady and the medications he took reduced his voice to a whisper, such that for years our conversations were mainly monologues, me trying to rehearse my doings in the hope of enlivening his increasingly restricted life. It was hard to hear him when he spoke: I see myself leaning close to his face with my ear at his parted lips, failing to catch what he was saying—if he was saying anything. I admit that I sometimes thought he was playing with me—that he would stop breathing entirely rather than speak the words I wanted to hear, whatever they were. "Whatever they were"—I wonder whether at some level I was hoping for words of approval, some sort of blessing.

The more I thought about Dad in the aftermath of reading Trillin, the more I realized how little I knew about him and what he wanted, how little he ever said to me about himself, his history, his feelings. But if the lesson of my difficulty in speaking about him that night at the wedding was how much unfinished business there was between us, how could I finish it now? Dad was above all a very private person: this was initially puzzling to me, given his reputation as outgoing; he was a fine public speaker whom people admired for his way with words and his wonderful stories and jokes (the only jokes I know are the ones he repeated over the years). This storytelling carried over into the tales he served up as memories. If we took him at his word, his had been a childhood out of James Whitcomb Riley, the folksy Hoosier poet—he was Riley's "barefoot boy with cheeks of tan." "When I was a boy," he would say, "I kept a little brush beside my bed up in the attic to brush the snow off my pillow." Of course I loved this fanciful stuff, and yet I came to see it and his polished public-speaking persona as a screen masking the private man who never talked to me about himself, his own story, his memories. There were so many things we never talked about.

To reconstruct the public man, what he had done and how he was known—and he *was* known, he was prominent in civic affairs—I tried to locate my copy of Dad's obituary. At first I couldn't find it, and later, when I did, it didn't tell me what I wanted to know. Pursuing his story, I reread the sections about him in my mother's memoir, an account of family history that I encouraged her to write and that we published privately in 1995. Now, ten years later, I felt as though I were reading these few paragraphs about Dad for the first time—I hung on every word. Strangely, I found my eyes were moist, even though my mother's account is so restrained—she always expressed what she saw and knew rather than what she felt. For example, this: "Paul had happy memories of summers in Crafton. He talked about a big white bulldog." Crafton? A white bulldog? Dad never that I could remember talked to me about his memories of anything.

My mother writes that Dad grew up "in a very church-oriented household." This is certainly an understatement, for spiritual exercises ran deep in his family. Dad's maternal grandfather, for example, "went every day to pray at a great rock in his orchard, weather permitting." Maybe you learn to keep things to yourself, I thought, when you grow up in a parsonage. "He went off to Muskingum, a small Presbyterian school," my mother continues, "at the age of 16 in his first pair of long pants. He was not invited to join any of the fraternities." Dad was that young! "After he graduated from Muskingum, he taught in a high school in Wauseon, Ohio, for a year to earn money to go to business school.... On election day he had a hard time concealing from fellow teachers the fact that he was not old enough to vote." In fact, Dad kept his youthful look all his life—even at an advanced age his face was comparatively unlined and rosy, his hair dark and abundant with only traces of gray.

My mother gets to the heart of Dad's story when she reports his idea of his career: "Paul had clearly defined life goals, to be highly successful in his field of investment counseling and to become a leading citizen in his community. I suppose one could say that he had achieved his goals before his illness brought a tragic end to his career. However, he was denied many years of productivity and enjoyment of the professional and civic prestige that he had earned. The diagnosis of Parkinson's disease was a devastating blow." It was certainly a blow to me in 1960—I was slow to recognize just how much of a blow to him. "He fought a courageous rear guard battle until unsuccessful surgery in 1963 destroyed all hope. After that his goals were gone." So Dad's goal-oriented story, which my mother tells as both one of success and also of failure, was playing out, had reached its end, just as I was setting out.

Thinking now about the surgery, which my mother presents as the abrupt, untimely conclusion of my father's story, I find it painful to think that I was so wrapped up in my own life or so much in denial about his condition that I never visited him during his extended stay in the hospital in New York—only a few hours away by train or car from Boston, where I was in graduate school. A prominent neurosurgeon had developed a startling technique to control the tremor and rigidity that are the hallmarks of Parkinson's disease by inserting dry ice directly into the brain. The procedure, daring and experimental, had produced significant benefits for some patients, and Dad must have been sufficiently desperate to take the chance. Why wasn't I there with him for the operation and afterward, I wonder. But I am not now the young man I was and that young man kept his distance.

I suspect that there were several things playing into my resistance; not just denial but also a kind of warning about what could happen to you if you got what you wanted.

Perhaps it was the thrust of Dad's ambition—not only for himself but for me—that made me uneasy. He had become a senior partner in an old-name East Coast investment banking firm, and he enjoyed the power and the status that went with it—the swank, exclusive places where his standing was recognized, the clubs where he was greeted by name. He had come a long way from Du Bois, Pennsylvania, where he was born, from Steubenville, Ohio, where he grew up. My brother says that Dad was in awe of what he had achieved from such small beginnings—"There's no position I couldn't have in Cleveland," Dad told him once. Did he really say that? It sounds like something out of Dreiser or Balzac. And he wanted me, the son of such a man, to be well-dressed at school—I remember him taking me to a tailor he knew, to be fitted out with the sort of topcoat that a boy like me should wear. Was I that kind of boy?

Searching my mother's memoir for clues about Dad, I began to doubt that I could find the answers to my questions in pages like these. Why hadn't I asked Dad about his life while he was still alive? All those unspoken things, that midwestern silence. Perhaps my lack of interest in his story back then had been a self-protective move, making space for myself and my own story. Was I so incurious, so self-involved, though, so oblivious to him and his needs, that I could fault him for failing to support me in my choice of career? At the very time that I was rising and expanding, starting to come into my own, his world was closing in: he had trouble walking, he was in a wheelchair, he struggled endlessly to be comfortable, and as my mother writes, he was never comfortable, he was engulfed by his malady, which increasingly kept him from ever speaking much at all. Didn't I owe him everything? Where would I have been without the education he pushed me to get? As it turned out, in the interview that landed me the job that I would keep for the rest of my life, the department chair noted that we were both graduates of the same schools, the ones my father's business partner had attended, the ones my father believed were so important for my future. So Dad's story for me has been my story after all in ways I didn't acknowledge when I wrote *Not a Story*. I was still fighting him off, or fighting free of him.

For years, ever since I began to identify my professional work as concerned with autobiography, why some people write it and why others read it, people would invariably ask me whether I had written my own autobiography. I would put them off by saying that I was a kind of crypto-autobiographer, someone who wrote his own story indirectly, obliquely, by writing about other people's lives. But why didn't I write my story? And then, too, there's the matter of all I didn't say when I *did* write it, however briefly. *Not a Story* indeed—fantastical, when I think of it, I who believe that what we are is very largely a function of the stories we tell about ourselves, I who claim to be writing a book about narrative identity. What, then, was holding me back from writing about my father? Well, to begin with, there was the illusion that there was nothing to say because Dad seemed to be an unknown quantity. There was also my uncomfortable feeling of inauthenticity, of lack, which my misgivings about vocation seemed to confirm. And then there was Dad's ill-ness, and my anxious thoughts that I might get it too. Hadn't I had a tremor in my hands ever since my café days in Paris? And deeper still, there was Dad's disquieting death, in 1980. It had not been a good death, and I had wanted to put it be-hind me. All these things enlarged the gulf between us that I couldn't bridge that night at the wedding. The blessing and the tremor: so being like Dad was good and also dangerous.

Here is a sentence that haunts me from my mother's memoir about Dad: "During summers when he was in college, he also sold brushes in little mining towns." Like Crafton and the white bulldog, it stands for all the stories he never told me. I see him alone somewhere, the young man on the road to success.

"Too late for stories now." Or so I said when I wrote *Not a Story*. I know better now. When my mother wrote that the failed brain surgery ended Dad's story in 1963—"after that his goals were gone"—she was only partly right. The suc-cess plot had run its course, for sure, but a father is always a father come what may. Fathers have plans for sons, and the sons know it. My mother and I both thought that Dad's story was over—over for him, maybe, but not for us.

The Pressure of Circumstances, the Power of Story

When I titled my micro-autobiography *Not a Story,* I im-plied not only that my own personal history was something

other than a story but that my account of it did not amount
to a story either. By the time I wrote "*My Father...*" three
years later, however, I had abandoned my anti-story posture.
No one stands free of life story models and the identities
they carry with them—who was I to think otherwise? The
idea that had sustained me growing up—that my "life" was
still waiting in the wings, that I would start to live it once
I had finished my education—struck me now as a comfortable, middle-class illusion. By contrast, Henry Mayhew's
little watercress girl was firmly anchored in her story at the
age of eight and knew it. No wonder, then, that Carolyn
Steedman's comments on this child made a deep impression
on me, for I at eight had been a stranger to such knowledge.
But there were other reasons that drew me to the little
watercress girl besides the iconic brevity of her story.

To begin with, her position in Mayhew's *London Labour
and the London Poor* made her an attractive symbol of
the individual's involvement in large-scale structures of
the state: embedded in the pages of that book, embedded
in culture. Then, too, that she should have the command
of self and story that Mayhew captures suggested that even
children, given the pressure of circumstances, can function
self-consciously as players in a narrative identity system;
they can know how to say who they are with the authority of an adult. I wrote in chapter 1 that through "memory
talk" parents and caregivers train children at a very early
age how to talk about themselves. Mayhew's child is older,
and working-class necessity has made her precociously
so; Mayhew reports that she "had entirely lost all childish

ways, and was, indeed, in thoughts and manner, a woman" (1:151). As the watercress seller comments, "I ain't a child"; she knows herself to be "one who's got a living and vittals to earn," someone with no time for playing in a park or spending coins on "sweet-stuff" (1:152).

Other pressures than those that follow from socioeconomic status can promote children's awareness of self and life-course. Lucy Grealy's *Autobiography of a Face,* for instance, portrays a young girl forced by a life-threatening cancer to contemplate deep questions about who she was and what her life would—or could—be like. Sometimes the catalyst for such self-recognition comes from within a child's family. The family may seek to impose its religious beliefs on its youngest members, for example, almost as a condition of belonging to the household—I am thinking of Richard Wright's puritanical grandmother in *Black Boy,* of Edmund Gosse's fundamentalist father in *Father and Son.* The collapse of family through death and divorce can be equally shaping. These days there seems to be no end to the proliferation of memoirs about dysfunctional families. Perhaps less numerous but increasingly prominent are the stories of children set adrift by war and the uprooting of peoples, such as Ishmael Beah's harrowing account of his life as a child soldier in *A Long Way Gone.*

Although other narratives would certainly have suggested other major factors—gender, for example, and race— that inflect the terms in which people think of themselves and their lives, class and the awareness of economic forces it generates seems to have been central to the five lives

I have presented in this chapter. Just as the watercress seller's working-class condition doubtless heightened her self-knowledge by propelling her at a painfully early age into the world of work, so my own protected middle-class position permitted an unusually belated entry into the world of work and delayed such recognitions. I think, though, that the lives of Marianne Gullestad's "everyday life philosophers" offer more-characteristic illustrations of the connection between socioeconomic status and self-awareness than either Mayhew's "Watercress Girl" narrative or my own. The three Norwegian contest autobiographers recall themselves as adolescents faced with life-course choices, and they reflect back now on the consequences of the decisions they made and did not make. I prefaced my discussion of Gullestad's fieldwork by invoking Michel de Certeau's leading questions about the everyday practices of individuals in contemporary consumer culture: "What do they make of what they 'absorb,' receive, and pay for? What do they do with it?" (31). Gullestad focuses on the values her autobiographers received, while I have targeted the models of self and life story coded in those value messages—"don't go too far," "reach out for something better," and so forth. I believe that Gullestad's case studies show the activity of making selves and life stories to be an everyday practice in Certeau's sense, one that is fundamental to social life today. In my account of what I called a narrative identity system in chapter 1 and again in my analysis of individualism in this present chapter, I have evoked a cultural context of constraint within which the individual's affirmation of identity—*I* write my story,

I say who I am—necessarily takes place. Carolyn Steedman's treatment of Mayhew's little watercress seller prompted me to ask, how can we discriminate agency from conditioning in this matter of identity? While it is not easy to assess the part of free will and the part of determinism in the playing out of our stories and our story-charged consciousnesses, I want to highlight the *act* of making life stories that yields the narrative identities we own to others when they ask us who we are. Here if anywhere is individualism's promise of freedom.

So what do people *do* with the story models they absorb? Two things: Gullestad's Norwegians report that they used them to structure their life-course decisions, and it is also true that they used them to structure the autobiographies they wrote for the "Write Your Life" contest. Life-course decisions, moreover, present themselves as choices of story lines, and they imply choices of identity as well. Einar, Kari, and Øivind make clear that they understand story and identity to be intimately linked in this way. Einar, for example, spells out this connection when he writes of his peers that "they went to school in order to 'become somebody,'" while he "was still at home and remained 'nobody'" (104); "I never made a career" (120). It is culture and its institutions (the family, the school, the church, and so forth) that teach the individual what lives look like, while it is the individual who *chooses* (or does not choose, and that is also a choice, as both Einar and Øivind confirm) to live a particular kind of life and become the person predicated by that life ("somebody" or "nobody").

Where should we locate this life-story-making, identity-conferring process? It is obviously a function of the performance of an identity narrative, and it is also a primary content of such a narrative, as the Norwegian stories show. It is always tempting to think that living a life would come before making a life story. That is why autobiography is so often thought of as an art of retrospect. But making autobiography turns out to be part of the fabric of our experience as we live it, as I mean to show in the next chapter in my investigation of autobiography's adaptive value. Insofar as this making involves a trying on of stories and their attendant identities, it is an art of the future, and it is always an act of self-determination no matter what the circumstances. Even Mayhew's little watercress seller, whose life chances were slim, got to have her say. Earlier in this chapter, sizing up Marianne Gullestad's "everyday" Norwegian lives, I wrote, "We never catch ourselves in the act of *becoming selves*." Knowing this full well, I nonetheless attempt in the next chapter to get at this fleeting process by way of an analysis of André Aciman's autobiographical sketch "Arbitrage." This brief essay not only creates a serviceable fiction that represents what identity construction might look like if we *could* witness it, but it suggests as well identity construction's enduring value as a source of meaning in our lives.

CHAPTER 4

LIVING AUTOBIOGRAPHICALLY

Waking at night in an old cabin on the shore of Lake Huron, I think how reassuring it is to know that I have a kind of built-in body map, keeping track of the position of my limbs in space, seeing to it that I don't roll over the edge of my high bed. This sets me thinking of that other map we consciously construct that charts our movement through time and the selves we have been at different moments along the way. Marcel Proust, of course, is the great precursor of night thoughts like these, and in the opening of *Swann's Way* he conjures up the map of our place in time that organizes our private worlds:

> When a man is asleep, he has in a circle round him the chain of the hours, the sequence of the years, the order of the heavenly host. Instinctively, when he awakes, he looks

to these, and in an instant reads off his own position on the earth's surface and the amount of time that has elapsed during his slumbers....

Then, continuing, Proust evokes the identity consequences triggered by disruptions in this temporal positioning system:

But for me it was enough if, in my own bed, my sleep was so heavy as completely to relax my consciousness; for then I lost all sense of the place in which I had gone to sleep, and when I awoke at midnight, not knowing where I was, I could not be sure at first who I was; I had only the most rudimentary sense of existence...but then the memory, not yet of the place in which I was, but of various other places where I had lived, and might now very possibly be, would come like a rope let down from heaven to draw me up out of the abyss of not-being, from which I could never have escaped by myself....

For Proust, the body, prompting memory, is central to this saving work of orientation, keeping us from falling out of our lives:

My body, still too heavy with sleep to move, would make an effort to construe the form which its tiredness took as an orientation of its various members, so as to induce from that where the wall lay and the furniture stood, to piece together and to give a name to the house in which it must be living.

On most nights, Proust suggests, we are anchored by our bodily knowledge of "the chain of the hours," "the order of the heavenly host"; and as for those other nights when the "ordered procession" of being becomes "confused," we can count on embodied memory to lift us from "the abyss of not-being" (1: 4–5).

Most of the time. But the day—the night—may come, sooner or later, when identity's memory-machine may cease to purr and its gears may start to slip. Then indeed the abyss of not-being into which Proust's narrator briefly slides may swallow us for good. This is the disorientation that threatens to turn longevity from a blessing into a nightmare—a nightmare, I grant, to which we may have become quite oblivious by the time it overtakes us, but a nightmare nonetheless for those intimates who rely on us to be the selves we have always, mostly, been. We need autobiography's identity work, we need its temporal tracking, and so, thinking about time and the body and about this notion of mapping, I want to revisit in this chapter a question that has fascinated me for nearly thirty years: Why do people tell and sometimes write their life stories? I have already proposed various answers in earlier chapters, but I want to make one more pass, with a view to suggesting that the memory work involved when we look back on our pasts is driven not only by our present circumstances but also by our plans for the future. Looking back, I see three stages in my thinking about the autobiographical act, a term that, after an initial infatuation, I began to think was rather pretentious. Now, in the light of neurobiology and brain studies, I find myself returning to it with new enthusiasm. Let me explain.

The Homeostatic Machine

What motivates us to tell and write the stories of our lives? My earliest answer to this question focused on individuals who claimed to write autobiography out of some irrepressible compulsion. I took Maxine Hong Kingston's girlhood self in *The Woman Warrior* as the prototype of the driven autobiographer. In Kingston's world, sanity and identity are linked to language, and the child-Maxine burns to break out of her conflicted silences in order to utter her experience, her self: "I had grown inside me a list of over two hundred things that I had to tell my mother so that she would know the true things about me and to stop the pain in my throat" (229). Frank Conroy, the author of *Stop-Time,* was another of the driven. "I have to write," he told an interviewer, "I would write even if I were strung up by my toes" (Midwood 152). Thinking about cases like these, I called the impulse to self-expression—rather grandly as it now seems to me—"the autobiographical imperative" (*Fictions in Autobiography* 275–78). I was drawn to the exceptional individual, to the romantic story of the artist.

Later on, following the lead of developmental psychologists, I traced the origins of autobiographical discourse to the young child's initiation into "memory talk." We learn as children what it means to say "I" in the cultures we inhabit, we learn to tell stories about ourselves, and this training proves to be crucial to the success of our lives as adults, for our recognition by others as normal individuals depends on our ability to perform the work of self-narration. As I argued in chapter 1, autobiographical discourse plays a decisive part in the regime of social accountability that governs our lives, and in this sense our identities could be said to be socially constructed and regulated.

This social perspective, however, leaves out of account the fact that our identities and identity narratives are rooted in our lives in and as bodies—this was my theme in chapter 2. The neurologist Antonio Damasio persuades me that our bodies can be said to have stories, and I want to argue now that the body's story not only serves as the substrate of the identity narratives we tell and write, but provides as well important insight into their function and value as maps of our lives in time. Let me rehearse Damasio's views briefly, drawing from two books, *The Feeling of What Happens: Body and Emotion in the Making of Consciousness* and *Looking for Spinoza: Joy, Sorrow, and the Feeling Brain.*

Our bodily existence is the central fact of our mental life. Damasio asserts that "the mind exists for the body, is engaged in telling the story of the body's multifarious events, and uses that story to optimize the life of the organism" (*Looking* 206). Not only do bodies have stories, then, but the telling of these stories has an adaptive value. In Damasio's usage, story or narrative denotes a biological process, the "imagetic representation of sequences of brain events" (*Feeling* 188) in prelinguistic "wordless stories about what happens to an organism immersed in an environment" (*Feeling* 189). The body's story is focused on *homeostasis,* a term Damasio employs as a "convenient shorthand for the ensemble of regulations and the resulting state of regulated life" in the human organism (*Looking* 30). From a neurobiological perspective, the body emerges as a "homeostasis machine" (*Looking* 31), and the body's homeostatic regulatory activities range from metabolism, basic reflexes, and the immune system at the lowest level, to pain and pleasure behaviors, drives and motivations, and finally to emotions and conscious feelings—the feelings that tell us that all these activities are taking place (*Looking* 31–37). The adaptive goal of all this manifold activity of homeostatic regulation, a great deal of it unconscious, is the well-being of the organism as it moves forward into the future. Damasio believes that "the continuous attempt at achieving a state of positively regulated life is a deep and defining part of our existence" (*Looking* 36). I would extend this view of the human organism's homeostatic regulatory activity to include our endless fashioning of identity narratives, our performance of the autobiographical act.

In Damasio's reckoning, autobiographical self and extended consciousness, to which the "I" of autobiography and memoir refers, are an integral part of the homeostatic machine that is the body. Is it far-fetched to align the events of our emotional, intellectual, and spiritual lives on a continuum with the microevents of our physiology, "the automatic regulation of temperature, oxygen concentration, or pH" (*Feeling* 39–40) in our bodies? Does it make sense to see the body's neurobiological story and the mind's psychological, social, and literary story as two different registers of a single narrative unfolding in the organisms that we are?[1]

---

1. The philosopher Ian Hacking, for one, does not think so. In a skeptical review of Damasio's work, Hacking contends that there is no place for the "I" in Damasio's model of the body's "self-regulating homeostasis" ("Minding the Brain"

What are the advantages to students of life writing in approaching autobiography in this way? We could say that autobiography's tracking of identity states across time serves a homeostatic goal. In this sense, the adaptive purpose of self-narrative, whether neurobiological or literary, would be the maintenance of stability in the human individual through the creation of a sense of identity. As self-narration maps and monitors the succession of body or identity states, it engenders "the notion of a bounded, single individual that changes ever so gently across time but, somehow, seems to stay the same" (*Feeling* 134). In particular—and this is the point I would like to explore in my discussion of the work of André Aciman—this homeostatic, regulatory perspective can sensitize us to the fact that autobiographical memory and autobiographical narrative are oriented to the future. Thinking about autobiography as an expression of homeostatic regulatory activity has given me a new sense of the interplay between past, present, and future in the autobiographical act.

Let me flash back to 1976, when I was studying Henry James's autobiography. No autobiographer ever wrote more self-consciously about self-consciousness than James did as he paced up and down in his workrooms in Chelsea and Rye, dictating the story of his life to an attentive typist. James's often flamboyant dramatization of the autobiographer engaged in the act of retrospect led me to the following conclusion:

---

36). From Hacking's reductive account, it would be impossible to guess that in fact Damasio has constructed an elaborate theory to show how consciousness and self emerge in the human organism.

> When we settle into the theater of autobiography, what we
> are ready to believe—and what most autobiographers en-
> courage us to expect—is that the play we witness is a histori-
> cal one, a largely faithful and unmediated reconstruction of
> events that took place long ago, whereas in reality the play is
> that of the autobiographical act itself, in which the materials
> of the past are shaped by memory and imagination to serve
> the needs of present consciousness. (*Fictions* 56)

Even though I have come to believe that autobiography's reconstructed story of the past always functions as a
metaphor for the story of that story, the story of the autobiographical act unfolding in the present, I also still believe
that autobiographers and their readers—and here I include
myself—continue to take for granted this expectation that
autobiography is devoted to the recovery of the past.

To Nick Carraway's assertion "You can't repeat the
past," I want to reply with Jay Gatsby, "Why of course you
can!"—at least in memory. Yet I know that we can't step
into the same river twice. Moreover, I suspect we *all* instinctively know this, which accounts for our thrill at the neurological "error" that yields the fleeting experience of déjà vu.
Analysis of memories as neurological events confirms that
even when we believe that we are recalling exactly the same
memory on a series of occasions, the brain constructs that
memory anew each time, with different centers of brain
activity involved in each occurrence.[2] Why *do* we buy in to
autobiography's retrospective illusion, the "you-are-there"

2. See, e.g., Rosenfield.

narratives, such as Frank McCourt's *Angela's Ashes,* that mask the autobiographical act unfolding in the present? To start with the obvious, it is because we are steadily moving away from the past into the future, and we want to bridge the gap. Also, and equally important, I think it is because the present is not a story yet. We can know it only indirectly, and we are conditioned socially—and I would speculate neurologically as well—to absorb our journey across time in narrative terms. (I am assuming here that narrative identity, while not the only manifestation of self-experience, is its preeminent form in the United States, as I argued in chapter 1. I like to think, though, that my analysis could apply in a good many other places as well.) And it is worth noting that even those autobiographers who do disclose the unfolding of the autobiographical act in the present, who tell us the story of their story, as Art Spiegelman does in *Maus* and as Christa Wolf does in *Patterns of Childhood,* tend to give it a narrative duration: it too has a trajectory stretching across time, such that the present of the autobiographical act in these cases is not a present of the present moment but rather a recent past, the history of the autobiography's composition.

What is new for me in Damasio's homeostatic angle is the role it suggests for the future in the work of memory. Here is Damasio commenting on the dynamic of time frames as they play out in the evolution of our autobiographical selves:

The changes which occur in the autobiographical self over an individual lifetime are not due only to the remodeling of the lived past that takes place consciously and unconsciously, but also to the laying down and remodeling of the anticipated future. I believe that a key aspect of self evolution concerns the balance of two influences: the lived past and the anticipated future. Personal maturity means that memories of the future we anticipate for the time that may lie ahead carry a large weight in the autobiographical self of each moment. The memories of the scenarios that we conceive as desires, wishes, goals, and obligations exert a pull on the self of each moment. No doubt they also play a part in the remodeling of the lived past, consciously and unconsciously, and in the creation of the person we conceive ourselves to be, moment by moment. (*Feeling* 224–25)

Years ago I observed that old Henry James used the story of his young self to "serve the needs of present consciousness." Damasio's comment makes me see that one of those "needs" is preparing for the future. Our desires and goals have embedded in them plots or "scenarios" for possible futures that motivate our recovery of the past. My hunch is that much of the time we don't quite see what this future might be, and that it is precisely by revisiting the past that the potential future comes into focus for us in the present. But even if we grant that young to midlife autobiographers on the order of Frank Conroy and Maxine Hong Kingston might be engaged in setting down "memories of the future," can we say the same of end-of-life players like James or Benjamin Franklin or W. Somerset Maugham? What future can be in question for them? The future of no future, we might say, or better still, we might remind ourselves, following

Erik Erikson, that identity formation is a lifelong process, and that the endgame has a story of its own to tell.

"Arbitrage": André Aciman and "Remembering Remembering"

"Memory is deeper than we are and has longer views. When it pricked us and set us on, it was the future it had in mind" (66). The Australian novelist David Malouf makes this startling observation at the end of his wonderful memoir about his childhood home in Brisbane, "12 Edmondstone Street." When I first read this, I understood why he believed that memory could never truly recover the past (although he had certainly done so to my readerly satisfaction), but I did not quite grasp what he meant about memory and the future. I liked the sound of it in something like the way I like John Ashbery's poetry, a liking unsupported by any ability on my part to spell out an interpretation. Now, though, in the wake of reading André Aciman's "Arbitrage," an autobio-graphical sketch that he published in the *New Yorker* in the summer of 2000, I do see the connection between autobio-graphical memory and the future more clearly. As a former graduate student at Harvard myself, I was primed to like Aciman's story about a graduate student at Harvard writ-ing a seminar paper on Wordsworth for a woman friend on a hot summer evening in Cambridge thirty years ago. If Malouf had convinced me that you couldn't repeat the past precisely because to do so you would have to "un-remember" all the experience that had colored your consciousness in the intervening years, Aciman made me feel you could. His Cambridge of the early '70s was really not so different from my own of ten years before.

But first a word about André Aciman. The dust jacket for *False Papers,* published in 2000, a collection of more than a dozen autobiographical essays, including "Arbitrage," reports: "André Aciman was born in Alexandria, raised in Egypt, Italy, and France, and educated at Harvard. A frequent contributor to *The New Yorker, The New York Review of Books, The New York Times, The New Republic,* and *Commentary,* he teaches literature at Bard and lives in Manhattan with his wife and three children." Aciman is best known for his memoir *Out of Egypt,* published in 1994, which tells the story of his early life growing up in Alexandria, ending with his family's forced exile from Egypt in 1965.

"Arbitrage" is a story about memory and writing, and writing about memory. The premise of this many-layered autobiographical piece is comparatively simple. It is late summer 1973, and Aciman is invited by a woman from his seminar to have tea with her in her studio. Once there, she suddenly remembers another appointment, and the disappointed young man settles instead for writing a paper for her on Wordsworth's "Tintern Abbey." (Would I have done the same, I wondered.) Finishing the paper, he is inspired to write a story of his own. And then, after finishing a draft of his story, he puts his tea mug in the sink and heads home. And that's it. How much can one make out of an evening like that? Well, if you are André Aciman, the answer is, plenty.

To begin with, the cup of tea the young woman prepares for Aciman before she leaves turns out to be a Proustian cup of tea; or more precisely, I should say that when she serves the tea, she places a quilted tea cozy over the pot, and it is this tea cozy that rings the Proustian changes:

> In the cloying comfort of the hot room, the presence of that unusual piece of quilting suddenly thrust me back a decade earlier, to the languid *fin d'été* world of my childhood in Alexandria, where I had lived before my family's expulsion, in 1965, and where my aging, after-school tutors had sipped tea at my desk. (34)

In this way the first of the series of epiphanies that stud this short narrative begins to cast its spell: "something in Wordsworth and me and this girl and this studio, and in my recognition now, years after reading Proust and Leopardi, of the unmistakable signals that a memory was just about to blossom there" (35). The complexity of "Arbitrage" stems from the many intricately interconnected layers of memory it subsequently deploys. The present of the story unfolds in 1973. Then there are Aciman's memories of the past prompted by the quilted tea cozy, including both his pre-1965 childhood in Alexandria and his years in Italy that followed from 1965 to 1968. Finally, there are his memories of the past that are the subject of the story he begins to write that summer evening in 1973, together with his memories of his subsequent rewritings of the story over the next two decades. So within the primary time frame of "Arbitrage," set in 1973, the autobiographer moves both backward to his youth and forward to the midlife retrospect behind the writing of "Arbitrage" more than twenty-five years later. A whole life is spanned in the compass of these few pages.

Aciman presents his theory of "arbitrage," his notion of memory's key orientation toward the future, in his analysis of Wordsworth's memory strategy in "Tintern Abbey"— the short form, as it were, of the spiritual autobiography he was to compose in *The Prelude*. Let me recall the movement of the poem briefly. In 1798 Wordsworth and his sister Dorothy visit the ruins of the abbey, which Wordsworth had visited five years earlier. The site is thus a memory site, prompting the poet's previous rememberings of his first visit and leading him to outline the stages of his evolving relation to nature up to the present moment. Complementing and completing this review of the past and the nurturing influence of nature's "beauteous forms" (22) is Wordsworth's analysis not only of the memory's contribution to his "present pleasure," but of its anticipated role in his future life: "pleasing thoughts/That in this moment there is life and food/For future years" (63–65). It is this orientation to the future that Aciman stresses in his commentary on Wordsworth's poem, which invokes "not only the present moment but also the previous visit, as well as the future memory of both visits." Aciman notes that Wordsworth "fears losing that future memory," and so he calls on Dorothy, should he die, "to remember their visit for him" (35).

Sensing an analogy between his own situation in Cambridge and Wordsworth's at Tintern Abbey, Aciman claims that they were both "firming up the present by experiencing it as a memory, by experiencing it from the future as a moment in the past." (Walt Whitman does this too, I might add, most notably in "Crossing Brooklyn Ferry." It could be that memory work of this kind is a characteristic feature of the romantic sensibility.) Aciman reads Wordsworth's memory work as follows: "What Wordsworth remembers at Tintern Abbey is not the past but himself in the past imagining the future; and what he looks forward to is not even the future but himself, in the future, retrieving the bone he buried in the past." In this wonderfully circular statement connecting present with past and future, the target of the poet's recall is not "the past" but self—self performing the act of recall. Aciman sees Wordsworth as practicing "mnemonic arbitrage," grounding "the present on the past, and the future on the past recaptured." Moreover, as Wordsworth makes clear in the poem, he had been practicing autobiographical arbitrage in this way ever since his first visit to Tintern Abbey. As Aciman puts it, "he was not just remembering. He was remembering remembering" (36).

The financial metaphor linking the memory work of Wordsworth and Aciman is apt, for the memory of place— whether a ruined abbey on the Wye or a Jewish cemetery in Alexandria, as we shall see—points up the investment of self in the act of memory. In "remembering remembering," it is traces of the self they seek to retrieve, self understood as the watermark of consciousness, that indelible signature that makes us recognize consciousness as our own. Aciman makes clear that it is memory itself, memory as act, "remembering remembering," rather than any of its possible contents, that is central to the recovery of self-experience. Thus he can say that "the very act of anticipating an epiphany becomes the epiphany itself" (36). Where Aciman speaks of epiphanies, Wordsworth speaks of "spots of time," but the double reference to future and to self is common to both writers. Wordsworth's "spots of time" possess "a vivifying Virtue" for the mind in the time to come, and yet it is the mind that stamps those "spots" and makes them what they are, "those passages of life in which/We have had deepest feeling that the mind/Is lord and master" (XI: 258, 260, 270–72). Living autobiographically, Wordsworth and Aciman are tracking this specular movement between self and place, charting self-experience. "If I keep writing about places," Aciman comments elsewhere, "it is because some of them are coded ways of writing about myself" ("Literary Pilgrim" 2).

Having finished the paper on "Tintern Abbey" for his friend, young Aciman begins to "write a story about going back to a place that was my own Tintern Abbey" (36), the Jewish cemetery in Alexandria where his grandfather is buried. Like Wordsworth at Tintern Abbey, Aciman's young man is revisiting a memory site. He recalls a visit he made ten years earlier with his father, and he also recalls subsequent memories of the cemetery and—associated with it—the beaches of Alexandria. Like Wordsworth, the young man is "remembering remembering." The story concludes when, in response to a hugely generous tip, the Bedouin cemetery warden who had helped him locate his grandfather's grave gives him "an antique silver cigarette lighter, with an inscription, probably left behind by a Jewish mourner years ago":

> To the young man's surprise, the inscription on the lighter bears all three of his initials. He knows that the lighter isn't his. He has never owned such a lighter. Had the other mourner left it for him? The young man had come to the cemetery not knowing that he was looking for something; this is what he found. (38)

Aciman's story, abbreviated to initials, is a story about self-discovery. It is also, and obviously, a fragment of auto-biography.

Looking back, and commenting on the "campy" epiphany he had "concocted" on that Cambridge summer night in 1973, Aciman writes: "The lighter could have belonged only to the young man—who was, of course, me. He/I *had* returned to the cemetery before, though we hadn't realized it. We had been going back there every day for years, leaving our lighter in the Bedouin's care to remind us that part of ourselves would be forever left behind in Egypt" (38). The aim, then, of "remembering remembering" is to invest place with self so that self can be extracted from place later on. The young man's lighter, like the "bone" Wordsworth had buried at Tintern Abbey, functions as the currency on Aciman's memory exchange. Lighter and bone are both counters for the commodity traded, traces of self. Elaborating on the young man's "mnemonic arbitrage," Aciman makes clear that his memory practices are intimately connected with writing autobiography: "In Alexandria, I was homesick for the place from which I had learned to re-create Alexandria, the way that the rabbis in exile were forced to reinvent their homeland on paper, only to find, perhaps, that they worshipped the paper more than the land" (37). Aciman gets it exactly right when he speaks of "remembering remembering": it is the act itself of remembering that is recalled—memory engaged, moreover, in the creation of the paper world of autobiography, for "Arbitrage" features the act of writing—and writing the paper on "Tintern Abbey," writing the story about the young man revisiting Alexandria, and writing "Arbitrage" about these writings are all acts of writing autobiography.

Aciman's autobiographies map his physical and mental journey, backward and forward, from place to place and time to time, and what he calls epiphanies function as the points of articulation in his memory system, sites from which he conjugates the time frames of self-experience, building a world to house his fleeting spirit, a world this exile can call home. But Aciman's view of the epiphanies that punctuate his experience and reveal to him its structure is quite ambivalent. While epiphanies are by definition positive, associated with moments of sudden revelation, the conclusion the young man "concocted" for his story—the gift of the lighter with the engraved initials—is indeed not only "campy" but inconclusive. Aciman reports that a nagging sense of something unfinished kept him working on the story for more than twenty years. This is hardly surprising given the logic of "remembering remembering," which teaches Aciman— and any autobiographer—that autobiography's true or real story is the story of the story, not the paper on "Tintern

Abbey," or the short story about the Jewish cemetery, but "Arbitrage," the narrative he published about all this writing in the *New Yorker*. "I loved summoning up the past more than I loved the past I summoned up," Aciman writes (38), wondering whether the autobiographical act, with its fancy footwork of temporal evocation, is not finally a form of evasion. He confesses that his "deepest fear of all," which came to him "obliquely" that summer night in 1973, "was of living directly under the noonday sun, without the shadows of past or future" (38–39), living, that is, without arbitrage. As to "the past," moreover: Is his paper Alexandria with its precious overlay of Proustian associations genuine or factitious? Doubting, Aciman pictures himself as "a dishonest guide who takes tourists to an archeological dig and then pretends to stumble on a statuette he has purposely planted there the day before" (38).

Then, in 1995, after the publication of his memoir *Out of Egypt,* Aciman returns to Alexandria, testing the city of his memory and imagination against the real thing. Revisiting the Jewish cemetery and locating his grandfather's grave, Aciman is primed for an epiphany. Ready to celebrate the rites of memory at its fountainhead, brimming with all the images and recollections of the years after he had left Egypt and the years before as well, Aciman experiences instead a letdown, as Wordsworth had before him—a kind of anti-epiphany. He recalls himself at his grandfather's grave:

> already sensing, as in the parable of the talents, that I had
> perhaps been a false steward for them, one who, as Words-
> worth describes in "The Prelude," "hath much received

and renders nothing back." I had stood and waited too long. Was this all I had to show for the years? All I could think of were Wordsworth's own words: *Was it for this?* ...I did not want to answer the question....I suddenly wished I were elsewhere again. (39)

He had wanted to "repatriate" his memories, but there proved to be no homecoming for them in Alexandria.

Aciman brings his essay in the *New Yorker* to a triumphant close with yet one more epiphany, making good on the homeostatic promise of memory's—and autobiography's—arbitrage. Returning to the narrative's opening frame in the young woman's studio apartment in Cambridge, he portrays his younger self as executing a dazzling, indeed heroic, homecoming. I want to quote from the final paragraph at some length to give the full flavor of Aciman's prose:

And, as I surveyed her room, I thought to myself that it would take very little to persuade me to wait for her, especially since she had said that I could, for I already knew not only that one day soon we would sleep together on this bed, between these sheets, but that on the night when that did happen I'd look back on this moment when I stood up from the table, feeling quite pleased with myself and, stepping toward her bed, swore to remember that, while thinking about Tintern Abbey and Alexandria and this girl and this bed and these sheets and everything else I wished to write about, I had also committed an act of arbitrage. I had marked this moment as one of those to which I knew I would return many times over, and not just on our first night together but in future years as well, and in other homes, perhaps with other women, and in other cities, because it was not even this moment, or this place, or this girl that mattered anymore, but how I had woven my desire to live and be happy with each, and that, even if nothing were to happen in my life to make me happy, the very act of thinking back on things could, in the end, make me no less happy than an experienced Ulysses, waking up in Ithaca, thinking of the journey home. (39)

In this founding myth of himself as the artist he was to become, Aciman recalls himself as a confident young man poised to come into his own, standing at the center and naming and claiming the materials of his world. In this magical moment, the young man setting out, looking forward, and the older man looking back, his journey done, are united as they both "remember remembering." Revisiting the past and surveying the present, the young man projects his future as a repetition of present consciousness. In this way, under the beneficent future-building regime of arbitrage, "the very act of thinking back on things" becomes for Aciman early and late the engine of a forward-looking odyssey of recollection that weighs equally in the balance with Ulysses' journey. The writer-to-be experiences a surge of creative power that displaces all his previous misgivings about himself as "dishonest guide," as "false steward," as failing to measure up to his opportunities. "It was for *this*"—he might now reply, as it were, to Wordsworth's disarming question—"it was for this act of arbitrage, this 'Arbitrage.'" The performance of memory work itself constitutes an epiphany: "I had marked this moment." Sometimes, miraculously, spontaneously, as in the moment of the Proustian tea cozy, our experience seems to come to us already marked and structured; sometimes, as in Aciman's acts of arbitrage, we mark it consciously and deliberately ourselves; and sometimes, more formally, we cast it into autobiography.

This moment of conscious marking, the prototype of the autobiographical act, is what I mean by living autobiographically. What Aciman gives shape to in this memorable passage, and indeed in "Arbitrage" as a whole, is the process of making identity narrative that we all engage in all the time. We tend to think of autobiography as something created after the fact, at one remove from the experience that is its subject, as something over and finished. But Aciman and Aciman's Wordsworth suggest that experience itself, especially in its acts of arbitrage when we remember remembering, is already autobiography in the making. And this making, this mapping of our lives in time, I like to think, helps us to keep track of who we are.

WORKS CITED

Aciman, André. "Arbitrage." *New Yorker,* 10 July 2000: 34–39.

———. *False Papers: Essays on Exile and Memory.* New York: Farrar, 2000.

———. "A Literary Pilgrim Progresses to The Past." *New York Times,* 28 Aug. 2000, National ed., sec. B: 1+.

———. *Out of Egypt: A Memoir.* New York: Farrar, 1994.

Adams, Henry. *The Education of Henry Adams.* 1907. Ed. Ernest Samuels. Boston: Houghton, 1973.

Ariès, Philippe. *Centuries of Childhood: A Social History of Family Life.* 1960. Trans. Robert Baldick. New York: Random, 1962.

Barthes, Roland. *Roland Barthes by Roland Barthes.* 1975. Trans. Richard Howard. New York: Farrar, 1977.

Battersby, James L. "Narrativity, Self, and Self-Representation." *Narrative* 14 (2006): 27–44.

Bayley, John. *Elegy for Iris.* New York: St. Martin's, 1999.

Beah, Ishmael. *A Long Way Gone: Memoirs of a Boy Soldier.* New York: Farrar, 2007.

Bertaux, Daniel, and Martin Kohli. "The Life Story Approach: A Continental View." *Annual Review of Sociology* 10 (1984): 215–37.

Blakeslee, Sandra. "Cells That Read Minds." *New York Times,* 10 Jan. 2006, National ed., sec. D: 1+.

Brooks, Peter. *Troubling Confessions: Speaking Guilt in Law & Literature.* Chicago: University of Chicago Press, 2000.

Bruner, Jerome. *Acts of Meaning.* Cambridge, MA: Harvard University Press, 1990.

Bruss, Elizabeth. *Autobiographical Acts: The Changing Situation of a Literary Genre.* Baltimore: Johns Hopkins University Press, 1976.

"Call It Fiction." *New York Times,* 13 Jan. 2006, National ed., sec. A: 22.

Cassidy, John. "Me Media." *New Yorker,* 15 May 2006: 50–59.

Certeau, Michel de. *The Practice of Everyday Life.* Trans. Steven F. Rendall. Berkeley: University of California Press, 1984.

Chaloupka, William. "(For)getting a Life: Testimony, Identity, and Power." In *Getting a Life: Everyday Uses of Autobiography.* Ed. Sidonie Smith and Julia Watson. Minneapolis: University of Minnesota Press, 1996. 369–92.

Conroy, Frank. *Stop-Time.* New York: Viking, 1967.

Couser, G. Thomas. "Crossing the Borderline (Personality): Madness Interrogated in *Girl, Interrupted.*" Paper given at American Literature Association conference on "American Autobiography." Cancún, Mexico, 10–11 Dec. 1999.

Crossen, Cynthia. "Know Thy Father." Rev. of *The Kiss,* by Kathryn Harrison. *Wall Street Journal,* 4 Mar. 1997, sec. A: 16.

Damasio, Antonio R. *Descartes' Error: Emotion, Reason, and the Human Brain.* 1994. New York: Avon, 1995.

———. *The Feeling of What Happens: Body and Emotion in the Making of Consciousness.* New York: Harcourt, 1999.

———. *Looking for Spinoza: Joy, Sorrow, and the Feeling Brain.* New York: Harcourt, 2003.

D'Souza, Dinesh. "I, Rigoberta Menchú … Not!" *Weekly Standard,* 28 Dec. 1998: 27–29.

Dowd, Maureen. "Oprah! How Could Ya?" *New York Times,* 14 Jan. 2006, National ed., sec. A: 31.

Eakin, Paul John. *Fictions in Autobiography: Studies in the Art of Self-Invention.* Princeton, NJ: Princeton University Press, 1985.

———. *How Our Lives Become Stories: Making Selves.* Ithaca, NY: Cornell University Press, 1999.

———. "Introduction: Mapping the Ethics of Life Writing." *The Ethics of Life Writing.* Ed. Paul John Eakin. Ithaca, NY: Cornell University Press, 2004. 1–16.

———. *Touching the World: Reference in Autobiography.* Princeton, NJ: Princeton University Press, 1992.

Edelman, Gerald M., and Giulio Tononi. *A Universe of Consciousness: How Matter Becomes Imagination.* New York: Basic, 2000.

Egan, Timothy. "Old, Ailing and Finally a Burden Abandoned." *New York Times,* 26 Mar. 1992, National ed., sec. A: 1+.

Eggers, Dave. *A Heartbreaking Work of Staggering Genius.* New York: Simon & Schuster, 2000.

Erikson, Erik H. *Childhood and Society.* New York: W. W. Norton, 1950.

Eskin, Blake. "Honor for Wilkomirski Puts Affair Under Analysis." *Forward,* 19 Mar. 1999: 1+.

———. "Wilkomirski Defends Holocaust Memoir." *Forward,* 16 Apr. 1999: 1.

———. "Wilkomirski's New Identity Crisis." *Forward,* 18 Sep. 1998: 1+.

———. "Wilkomirski's Tale Takes New Turns Toward Bizarre." *Forward,* 15 Oct. 1999: 1+.

"A Few Little Pieces." *New York Times,* 3 Nov. 2007, National ed., sec. A: 20.

Fitzgerald, F. Scott. *The Crack-Up.* Ed. Edmund Wilson. 1945. New York: New Directions, 1956.

Fivush, Robyn. "The Functions of Event Memory: Some Comments on Nelson and Barsalou." In *Remembering Reconsidered: Ecological and Traditional Approaches to the Study of Memory.* Ed. Ulric Neisser and Eugene Winograd. New York: Cambridge University Press, 1988. 277–82.

———, and Elaine Reese. "The Social Construction of Autobiographical Memory." In *Theoretical Perspectives on Autobiographical Memory.* Ed. Martin A. Conway, David C. Rubin, Hans Spinnler, and Willem A. Wagenaar. Dordrecht, Netherlands: Kluwer Academic Publishers, 1992. 115–32.

Fleishman, Avrom. *Figures of Autobiography: The Language of Self-Writing in Victorian and Modern England.* Berkeley: University of California Press, 1983.

Foucault, Michel. *The Birth of the Clinic: An Archaeology of Medical Perception.* Trans. A. M. Sheridan Smith. New York: Pantheon, 1973.

———. *Discipline and Punish: The Birth of the Prison.* 1975. Trans. Alan Sheridan. New York: Pantheon, 1977.

Franzen, Jonathan. "My Father's Brain." *How to Be Alone: Essays.* New York: Picador, 2003. 7–38.

Frey, James. *A Million Little Pieces.* New York: Doubleday, 2003.

Gazzaniga, Michael S. *The Ethical Brain: The Science of Our Moral Dilemmas.* 2005. New York: Harper Perennial, 2006.

Geertz, Clifford. "From the Native's Point of View: On the Nature of Anthropological Understanding." In *Meaning in Anthropology.* Ed. Keith H. Basso and Henry A. Selby. Albuquerque: University of New Mexico Press, 1976. 221–37.

———. *The Interpretation of Cultures.* New York: Basic, 1973.

Gladwell, Malcolm. "Damaged." *New Yorker,* 24 Feb.-3 Mar. 1997: 132–47.

Gosse, Edmund. *Father and Son: A Study of Two Temperaments.* London: Heinemann, 1907.

Gourevitch, Philip. "The Memory Thief." *New Yorker,* 14 June 1999: 48–68.

Grady, Denise. "At Life's End, Many Patients Are Denied Peaceful Passing." *New York Times,* 29 May 2000, National ed., sec. A: 1+.

Grealy, Lucy. *Autobiography of a Face.* Boston: Houghton, 1994.

Gullestad, Marianne. *Everyday Life Philosophers: Modernity, Morality, and Autobiography in Norway.* Oslo: Scandinavian University Press 1996.

——. "Reflections of an Anthropologist Commuter." *The Art of Social Relations: Essays on Culture, Social Action and Everyday Life in Modern Norway.* Oslo: Scandinavian University Press, 1992. 1–33.

——, and Reidar Almås. "Write Your Life: A Norwegian Life Story Contest." *Oral History* 20 (1992): 61–65.

Hacking, Ian. "The Looping Effects of Human Kinds." In *Causal Cognition: A Multidisciplinary Debate.* Ed. Dan Sperber, David Premack, and Ann James Premack. Oxford: Clarendon, 1995. 351–83.

——. "Making Up People." In *Reconstructing Individualism: Autonomy, Individuality, and the Self in Western Thought.* Ed. Thomas C. Heller, Morton Sosna, and David E. Wellbery. Stanford, CA: Stanford University Press, 1986. 222–36.

——. "Minding the Brain." *New York Review of Books,* 24 June 2004: 32–36.

——. "Normal People." In *Modes of Thought: Explorations in Culture and Cognition.* Ed. David R. Olson and Nancy Torrance. Cambridge: Cambridge University Press, 1996. 59–71.

Harrison, Colin. "Sins of the Father." *Vogue,* Apr. 1997: 328+.

Harrison, Kathryn. *The Kiss.* New York: Random, 1997.

Hartman, Geoffrey. "The Humanities of Holocaust Testimony." Paper presented at "Autobiography Across the Disciplines" conference. Whitney Humanities Center, Yale University, 29 Oct. 2005.

Horgan, John. "More than Good Intentions: Holding Fast to Faith in Free Will." *New York Times,* 31 Dec. 2002, National ed., sec. D: 3.

James, William. *The Principles of Psychology.* 2 vols. New York: Henry Holt, 1890.

Kakutani, Michiko. "Bending the Truth In a Million Little Ways." *New York Times,* 17 Jan. 2006, National ed., sec. B: 1+.

Karr, Mary. "His So-Called Life." *New York Times,* 15 Jan. 2006, National ed., sec. 4: 13.

——. *The Liars' Club.* New York: Viking, 1995.

Kaysen, Susanna. *Girl, Interrupted.* 1993. New York: Random, 1994.

Kennedy, Randy. "My True Story, More or Less, And Maybe Not at All." *New York Times,* 15 Jan. 2006, National ed., sec. 4: 1+.

Kermode, Frank. *The Sense of an Ending: Studies in the Theory of Fiction.* New York: Oxford University Press, 1968.

Kingston, Maxine Hong. *The Woman Warrior: Memoirs of a Girlhood Among Ghosts.* New York: Knopf, 1976.

Kraft, Robert N. *Memory Perceived: Recalling the Holocaust.* Westport, CT: Praeger, 2002.

Lakoff, George, and Mark Johnson. *Metaphors We Live By.* Chicago: University of Chicago Press, 1980.

———. *Philosophy in the Flesh: The Embodied Mind and Its Challenge to Western Thought.* New York: Basic, 1999.

Lappin, Elena. "The Man with Two Heads." *Granta* 7, no. 66 (1999): 8–65.

Lejeune, Philippe. "Archives autobiographiques." *Le débat* 54 (mars-avril 1989): 68–76.

———. "L'atteinte à la vie privée." *Pour l'autobiographie: chroniques.* Paris: Seuil, 1998. 69–74.

———. "The Autobiographical Pact." In *On Autobiography.* Ed. Paul John Eakin. Trans. Katherine Leary. Minneapolis: University of Minnesota Press, 1989. 3–30.

———. *Cher écran: journal personnel, ordinateur, Internet.* Paris: Seuil, 2000.

———. "Les instituteurs du XIXe siècle racontent leur vie." *Histoire de l'éducation* 25 (janvier 1985): 53–104.

———. *Moi aussi.* Paris: Seuil, 1986.

Levy, Steven. "Dr. Edelman's Brain." *New Yorker,* 2 May 1994: 62–73.

Linde, Charlotte. *Life Stories: The Creation of Coherence.* New York: Oxford University Press, 1993.

McCourt, Frank. *Angela's Ashes: A Memoir.* New York: Scribner's, 1996.

MacFarquhar, Larissa. "The Bench Burner." *New Yorker,* 10 Dec. 2001: 78–89.

Macpherson, C. B. *The Political Theory of Possessive Individualism: Hobbes to Locke.* Oxford: Clarendon, 1962.

Maechler, Stefan. *The Wilkomirski Affair: A Study in Biographical Truth.* New York: Schocken, 2001.

Malouf, David. "12 Edmondstone Street." In *12 Edmondstone Street.* Ringwood, Victoria: Penguin, 1986. 1–66.

Marcus, Steven. "Freud and Dora: Story, History, Case History." *Partisan Review* 41 (1974): 12–23, 89–108.

Maxwell, William. *So Long, See You Tomorrow.* New York: Knopf, 1980.

Mayhew, Henry. *London Labour and the London Poor.* 4 vols. 1861–62. New York: Dover, 1968.

Menchú, Rigoberta. *I, Rigoberta Menchú: An Indian Woman in Guatemala.* 1983. Ed. and intro. Elisabeth Burgos-Debray. Trans. Ann Wright. New York: Verso, 1984.

Michaels, S. "The Dismantling of Narrative." In *Developing Narrative Structure.* Ed. A. McCabe and A. Peterson. Hillsdale, NJ: Erlbaum, 1991. 303–51.

Midwood, Barton. "Short Visits with Five Writers and One Friend." *Esquire,* Nov. 1970: 150–53.

Miller, Peggy J. "Instantiating Culture through Discourse Practices: Some Personal Reflections on Socialization and How to Study It." In *Ethnography and Human Development: Context and Meaning in Social Inquiry.* Ed. Richard Jessor, Anne Colby, and Richard A. Schweder. Chicago: University of Chicago Press, 1996. 183–204.

——, and Lisa Hoogstra. "Language as a Tool in the Socialization and Apprehension of Cultural Meanings." In *New Directions in Psychological Anthropology.* Ed. Theodore Schwartz, Geoffrey M. White, and Catherine A. Lutz. New York: Cambridge University Press, 1992. 83–101.

——, Angela R. Wiley, Heidi Fung, and Chung-Hui Liang. "Personal Storytelling as a Medium of Socialization in Chinese and American Families." *Child Development* 68 (1997): 557–68.

"A Nation Challenged: Portraits of Grief." *New York Times,* 31 Dec. 2001, National ed., sec. B: 6–7.

Needham, Rodney. "Inner States as Universals: Sceptical Reflections on Human Nature." In *Indigenous Psychologies: The Anthropology of the Self.* Ed. Paul Heelas and Andrew Lock. London: Academic, 1981. 65–78.

Neisser, Ulric. "Five Kinds of Self-Knowledge." *Philosophical Psychology* 1 (1988): 35–59.

Nelson, Katherine. *Language in Cognitive Development: Emergence of the Mediated Mind.* New York: Cambridge University Press, 1996.

Parker, David. *The Self in Moral Space: Life Narrative and the Good.* Ithaca, NY: Cornell University Press, 2007.

Porter, Roy. *A Social History of Madness: The World through the Eyes of the Insane.* New York: Weidenfield and Nicolson, 1987.

Posner, Richard A. "An Economic Theory of Privacy." 1978. In *Philosophical Dimensions of Privacy: An Anthology.* Ed. Ferdinand David Schoeman. Cambridge: Cambridge University Press, 1984. 333–45.

Prosser, William L. "Privacy." 1960. In *Philosophical Dimensions of Privacy: An Anthology.* Ed. Ferdinand David Schoeman. Cambridge: Cambridge University Press, 1984. 104–55.

Proust, Marcel. *Swann's Way. The Remembrance of Things Past.* Trans. C. K. Scott Moncrieff. 2 vols. New York: Random, 1934.

Rachels, James, and William Ruddick. "Lives and Liberty." In *The Inner Citadel: Essays on Individual Autonomy.* Ed. John Christman. New York: Oxford University Press, 1989. 221–33.

Raines, Howell. "Interview with Robert Siegel." *All Things Considered:* National Public Radio, 31 Dec. 2001.

"Revisiting the Families." *New York Times,* 11 Sept. 2006, National ed., sec. A: 14–15.

Rich, Frank. "Truthiness 101: From Frey to Alito." *New York Times,* 22 Jan. 2006, National ed., sec. 4: 16.

Rich, Motoko. "Publisher and Author Settle Suit Over Lies." *New York Times,* 7 Sept. 2006, National ed., sec. B: 1.

Ricoeur, Paul. *Time and Narrative.* 3 vols. Trans. Kathleen McLaughlin and David Pellauer. Chicago: University of Chicago Press, 1984–88.

Riesman, David, Reuel Denney, and Nathan Glazer. *The Lonely Crowd: A Study of the Changing American Character.* New Haven, CT: Yale University Press, 1950.

"Riverhead Books Pulls Out of James Frey Deal." *New York Times,* 24 Feb. 2006, National ed., sec. B: 4.

Rohter, Larry. "Nobel Winner Accused of Stretching Truth." *New York Times,* 15 Dec. 1998, National ed., sec. A: 1+.

Roos, J. P. "Life Stories of Social Changes: Four Generations in Finland." *International Journal of Oral History* 6 (1985): 179–90.

Rosen, Jeffrey. "The Trials of Neurolaw." *New York Times Magazine,* 11 Mar. 2007: 48+.

Rosenfield, Israel. *The Invention of Memory: A New View of the Brain.* New York: Basic, 1988.

Rybczynski, Witold. *Home: A Short History of an Idea.* New York: Viking, 1986.

Sacks, Oliver. "Making up the Mind." *New York Review of Books,* 8 Apr. 1993: 42–49.

——. *The Man Who Mistook His Wife for a Hat.* 1985. New York: Harper, 1987.

St. John, Warren. "Kathryn Harrison's Dad Responds to Her Memoir." *New York Observer,* 21 Apr. 1997: 1+.

Sartre, Jean-Paul. *The Words.* Trans. Bernard Frechtman. New York: G. Braziller, 1964.

Schacter, Daniel L. *Searching for Memory: The Brain, the Mind, and the Past.* New York: Basic, 1996.

Searle, John R. "The Mystery of Consciousness." *New York Review of Books,* 2 Nov. 1995: 60–66.

——. "The Mystery of Consciousness: Part 2." *New York Review of Books,* 16 Nov. 1995: 54–61.

Sheringham, Michael. *Everyday Life: Theories and Practices from Surrealism to the Present.* Oxford: Oxford University Press, 2006.

Shotter, John. "Social Accountability and the Social Construction of 'You.'" In *Texts of Identity.* Ed. John Shotter and Kenneth J. Gergen. London: Sage, 1989. 133–51.

Smith, Sidonie. "Taking It to a Limit One More Time: Autobiography and Autism." In *Getting a Life: Everyday Uses of Autobiography.* Ed. Sidonie Smith and Julia Watson. Minneapolis: University of Minnesota Press, 1996. 226–46.

Spiegelman, Art. *Maus I: A Survivor's Tale: My Father Bleeds History.* New York: Pantheon, 1986.

———. *Maus II: A Survivor's Tale: And Here My Troubles Began.* New York: Pantheon, 1991.

Spolsky, Ellen. *Gaps in Nature: Literary Interpretation and the Modular Mind.* Albany, NY: State University Press of New York, 1993.

———. "Preface." *The Work of Fiction: Cognition, Culture, and Complexity.* Ed. Alan Richardson and Ellen Spolsky. Aldershot, Hampshire: Ashgate, 2004. vii–xiii.

Steedman, Carolyn Kay. *The Tidy House: Little Girls Writing.* London: Virago, 1982.

———. *Landscape for a Good Woman: A Story of Two Lives.* 1986. New Brunswick, NJ: Rutgers University Press, 1987.

Stern, Daniel N. *The Interpersonal World of the Infant: A View from Psychoanalysis and Developmental Psychology.* New York: Basic, 1985.

Stoll, David. *Rigoberta Menchú and the Story of All Poor Guatemalans.* Boulder, CO: Westview Press, 1999.

Stone, Lawrence. *The Family, Sex and Marriage in England, 1500–1800.* New York: Harper, 1977.

Strawson, Galen. "Against Narrativity." *Ratio* 17 (2004): 428–52.

"Studio Has Second Thoughts About James Frey Memoir." *New York Times,* 30 Jan. 2006, National ed., sec. B: 2.

Sutton, Peter C. "Love Letters: Dutch Genre Paintings in the Age of Vermeer." In *Love Letters: Dutch Genre Paintings in the Age of Vermeer.* Greenwich, CT: Bruce Museum of Arts and Science, 2003. 14–49.

"A Taste for Fine Wine, a Seeker of Good Deals, and Fun on Halloween." Portraits of Grief. *New York Times,* 17 Nov. 2001, National ed., sec. B: 10.

Taylor, Charles. *Sources of the Self: The Making of the Modern Identity.* Cambridge, MA: Harvard University Press, 1989.

Trillin, Calvin. *Messages from My Father.* New York: Farrar, 1996.

———. *Remembering Denny.* New York: Farrar, 1993.

Trilling, Lionel. *Sincerity and Authenticity.* Cambridge, MA: Harvard University Press, 1972.

Updike, John. *Self-Consciousness: Memoirs*. New York: Knopf, 1989.

Wallen, Jeffrey. "Autobiography on the Internet: Representations of Self in a Posthuman Era." Paper presented at the Center for Literary and Cultural Studies, Harvard University, 22 April 2003.

Warhol, Robyn R., and Helena Michie. "Twelve-Step Teleology: Narratives of Recovery/Recovery as Narrative." In *Getting a Life: Everyday Uses of Autobiography*. Ed. Sidonie Smith and Julia Watson. Minneapolis: University of Minnesota Press, 1996. 327–50.

Warren, Samuel D., and Louis D. Brandeis. "The Right to Privacy." 1890. In *Philosophical Dimensions of Privacy: An Anthology*. Ed. Ferdinand David Schoeman. Cambridge: Cambridge University Press, 1984. 75–103.

Wegner, Daniel M. *The Illusion of Conscious Will*. Cambridge, MA: MIT Press, 2002.

Weintraub, Karl J. "Autobiography and Historical Consciousness." *Critical Inquiry* 1 (1975): 821–48.

White, Hayden. *The Content of the Form: Narrative Discourse and Historical Representation*. Baltimore: Johns Hopkins University Press, 1987.

Wiley, Angela R., Amanda J. Rose, Lisa K. Burger, and Peggy J. Miller. "Constructing Autonomous Selves through Narrative Practices: A Comparative Study of Working-Class and Middle-Class Families." *Child Development* 69 (1998): 833–47.

Wilkomirski, Binjamin. *Fragments: Memories of a Wartime Childhood*. 1995. Trans. Carol Brown Janeway. New York: Schocken, 1996.

Wolf, Christa. *Patterns of Childhood*. 1976. Trans. Ursule Molinaro and Hedwig Rappolt. New York: Farrar, 1980.

Wordsworth, William. *The Prelude or Growth of a Poet's Mind*. 1805. Ed. Ernest de Selincourt. 2nd ed. Oxford: Clarendon Press, 1959.

Wright, Richard. *Black Boy: A Record of Childhood and Youth*. New York: Harper, 1945.

Wyatt, Edward. "Best-Selling Memoir Draws Scrutiny." *New York Times*, 10 Jan. 2006, National ed., sec. B: 1+.

——. "Live on 'Oprah,' a Memoirist Is Kicked Out of the Book Club." *New York Times*, 27 Jan. 2006, National ed., sec. A: 1+.

——. "When A Memoir And Facts Collide." *New York Times*, 11 Jan. 2006, National ed., sec. B: 1+.

——. "Writer Says He Made Up Some Details." *New York Times*, 12 Jan. 2006, National ed., sec. A: 20.

Young, Kay, and Jeffrey L. Saver. "The Neurology of Narrative." Paper presented at the Modern Language Association convention. New York, 29 Dec. 1995.

INDEX